ALCATRAZ:
My Home Town

A memoir of my childhood
growing up on "The Rock"

ALCATRAZ:
My Home Town

A memoir of my childhood
growing up on "The Rock"

By Haroldene "Dena" Henry Freeman

American Ghost Media
Santa Monica, CA

ALCATRAZ:
My Home Town

Published by

American Ghost Media
Santa Monica, CA 90405

www.AmericanGhostMedia.com

Book Design By David Pisarra
Cover Design By Timm Freeman
www.TimmFreeman.com

Copyright © 2019 Haroldene "Dena" Freeman

All Rights Reserved. No part of this book may be reproduced, scanned or distributed in any printed or electronic form without the prior written permission of the author. Please do not participate in or encourage piracy of copyrighted materials in violation of the author's rights.

Printed in the United States of America

November 2019
First Edition
ISBN: 978-0-9994672-7-5

Contents

Foreword	i
Greyhound Bus Trip	1
Return to California	7
Alcatraz Halloween Party	17
Day Two on Alcatraz	27
More Family	33
The Little White Cottage Days	49
Santa Claus Lives on Alcatraz	57
Early 1946	65
The Alcatraz Riot of 1946	71
What the Dads Did	87
Another Move	95
Stay at the Stites' Farm	103
Windy, My Pet Pigeon	113
The Bicycle	121
Changing	131
Early Teen Years	139
The Bench	147
Teen Social Life	157

A Larger World	171
New Friends	183
Room for One More	189
Summer of 1953	199
Senior Year at Galileo High School	207
The Alcatraz Alumni Association	213
Conclusion	215

FOREWORD

Dear Reader,

Yes, there were families on Alcatraz Island while it was a Federal Prison. We were in a very close-knit community.

My father was a Correctional Officer. He believed his job was to teach the inmates different skills, so when they got out of prison, they had a way to make a living.

As kids, we all took the boat across San Francisco Bay to Pier 4 at the bottom of Van Ness Avenue and walked to school every morning and returned every afternoon on the three-thirty or the five o'clock boat. The trip was only ten minutes.

We played on the boat, on the parade ground, in the sandbox, at each other's houses and sometimes, alone.

Alcatraz was a wonderful place for me when I was growing up and I believe most of my friends would agree.

At any given time, there were about seventy kids living on Alcatraz with their families.

As you read this book you will learn about our little community.

Most of the books written about Alcatraz are about the prisoners. This book is about the people who lived there.

I hope you enjoy "Alcatraz, My Home Town."

Haroldene "Dena" Henry Freeman

GREYHOUND BUS TRIP

My brother Bobby and I had been living on Campbell's Poultry Farm for two years. She and Zollie, my stepfather, had a baby in September of 1942. We called our baby sister "Skookie."

Summertime of 1943, and we had chores to do and a two-year-old little sister to take care of. Zollie and She worked at the Air Force Base. She worked in the commissary butcher shop. Zollie worked in base construction. They were gone from early morning until after five in the afternoon.

It must have been a Saturday because both She and Zollie were home. This was the evening milking time. Bobby and I were out in the shed, getting ready to milk the cow. Bobby had helped lead the cow into the shed and over to the feeding trough. He moved the piece of wood that held the cows' head in place over the alfalfa. The cow began to eat.

He had just grabbed the milking stool and the bucket and was about to sit when the cow lifted her right hind leg and stepped right on the top of Bobby's left foot. He let out a cry and hit her. When he withdrew his foot, there was blood coming from the center of the dark black mole just above his left little toe.

He ran up to the house, crying all the way.

I stayed behind to milk the cow. I was seven years old and remember having to milk the cow since early in the time of living with Her and Zollie. Upon finishing the milking, I stripped the teats and patted the cow firmly, as I moved the bar to allow her to leave the milking stall.

When I got the bucket of milk to the old adobe farmhouse, She was waiting to pour it into a big gallon jar. It would sit in the jar for some time, to allow the cream to rise to the top.

Bobby was sitting in the living room with his legs up on the couch and a bandage over his left foot injury.

After dinner, She would put Skookie to bed. Then She and Zollie would listen to the radio and read. The routine was seldom changed. Bobby and I got to play outside until it was dark.

Over the next year, Bobby and I went to school during the fall and spring semesters. Skookie went to a daycare center, which was in the town of Douglas. I spent most of the spring semester in the coatroom because I punched a girl, from an upper grade, for saying something bad about someone else while we were on the playground.

It was mid-summer, when She packed the suitcases and told us we were going to visit her friends, the Arps, in Inglewood, California.

The Greyhound bus was crowded. Almost every seat was filled. A lot of men in uniform were on the bus. Bobby and I sat on the long seat at the very back of the bus. We could whisper quietly and when the road got bumpy, we liked the bumps. The trip lasted all night and much of the next day. At a high point in the trip, hours after leaving Yuma, Bobby and I could see the Pacific Ocean from the backseat of the bus as it drove over a hilltop, toward the west.

Mrs. Arp was at the bus station in Los Angeles. When we got off the bus, Mrs. Arp waited with Bobby and me, while She got the suitcases from the baggage window. We all left the station together and caught a streetcar headed south from L.A. central.

The tall buildings, the numbers of cars and the noise were all new to us. When we got off the trolley, we still had to walk several blocks to get to the house where Mr. and Mrs. Arp lived.

As soon as we walked into the living area, there was Mr. Arp. I didn't want to be anywhere close to him. Bobby and I had compared body parts. Now I knew that the "soft flashlight" in Mr. Arp's coveralls was not a "flashlight" at all.

Mr. Arp used to have me sit on his lap, when the women were downtown, in Douglas, shopping. He would have me squeeze the "soft flashlight to make it hard." He was not a nice man.

Bobby and I met some of the other kids along the block. The morning after we arrived, we were playing hopscotch on the sidewalk when a man dressed in a suit and a hat passed, going toward the Arps home.

Soon after he passed, She called us to come in.

During this time in our history, children did not speak unless spoken to. I stood near the knees of the suited man, as he sat in an overstuffed chair, in the living area. He asked if I wanted to sit on his lap. I turned my back to him and he lifted me onto his lap. It was then that I heard him swallow. I have no idea why, but that is the moment when I said, "You're my father!"

He said he was and he seemed pleased.

The grownups talked and talked. After a time, She asked Bobby to show Pop his left little toe and the dark black mole that was growing.

As Bobby showed his toe, She told the story of the cow stepping on the mole. She reported that the mole had been growing since that time. Pop appeared very concerned.

About then, a plan was made for Bobby to go with Pop, up to San Francisco, for grandfather to examine the mole. Grandfather was a doctor and had connections with other doctors in the big city.

Pop stayed for dinner at the Arps. After dinner, She and Pop went somewhere while Bobby and I stayed to play outside until dark.

Mrs. Arp told us to get ready and go to bed. Bobby and I were to sleep in one of the twin beds in a bedroom. She would sleep in the other bed, when she got back from being with Pop. This bedroom connected to a bathroom, right off the living area.

We were laying in the twin bed, whispering about Bobby going to San Francisco with Pop the next day. The room was pretty dark. The bathroom door opened softly and there, silhouetted by the bathroom light, stood Mr. Arp. He was naked. We could not see his face. We could tell that he was playing with his penis and moving his hand faster and faster until he shut the door and left the room in darkness. He was not a nice man.

The following morning, Bobby and I had cold cereal for breakfast, and then went out on the sidewalk to play with the other kids.

Pop came to get Bobby about noontime. Bobby was being very brave. He did not know our father and was not sure what awaited him. She and Pop told him that grandfather Henry was expecting them and he couldn't disappoint him.

She, the Arps and I all went out on the sidewalk to wave goodbye to them. I waved until I couldn't see them anymore. They were going to catch the streetcar, which headed for the Los Angeles Greyhound Bus terminal.

After dinner, on that same day, She repacked the suitcase. She and I said our goodbyes to the Arps as we left for the streetcar, which went to the same Los

ALCATRAZ: My Home Town

Angeles Greyhound Bus station. It was not a long wait before She and I boarded the bus headed back to Douglas, Arizona and Campbell's Poultry Farm.

RETURN TO CALIFORNIA

Bobby was still in San Francisco with our father. I missed Bobby the most during the hot summer days on the poultry farm where I now had most of the chores to do by myself.

I had flunked third grade and I was not looking forward to the beginning of school after Labor Day.

Skookie was two and a half years old. She was talking very well and was in toilet training. On a Saturday, Skookie was playing out in front of the old adobe farmhouse in her little white cotton panties. It was warm enough that she needed no other clothing. The mallard ducks followed her as she threw hands full of grain to them.

It was then that She noticed the bulge in the back of Skookie's panties. She came out the kitchen door and walked quickly toward my baby sister. She pulled down the little white panties and took hold of the little brown turd. She angrily turned Skookie to face Her and forced my baby sister to take a bite of the brown, stinky turd.

ALCATRAZ: My Home Town

She screamed at the tiny little girl, "That'll teach you not to poop your pants."

My baby sister looked frightened and began to cry. She grabbed her by the hand and walked quickly to the house, forcing the little one to almost run to keep up with Her long strides.

I stayed quiet while continuing to feed the white ducks in the pens near the front of the house. Time had taught me to stay away from Her when She was angry.

Skookie was still going to the daycare center during the week. She was home on the poultry farm when all the rest of us were.

My little sister was learning how to climb out of her crib now. Even at a young age, Skookie had learned not to climb out unless She had given permission.

She packed the suitcases again. On the way to the Greyhound Bus station, She and Zollie took Skookie into her grandmother's house, while I waited in the back of the Dodge pickup. Nana was going to take care of my baby sister and cook dinner for Zollie until She was back from the trip to San Francisco.

This time, it was just She and I who got on the Greyhound Bus at the station in Douglas. It was late afternoon or early evening when the bus pulled out of Douglas and headed west toward the Pacific Ocean.

With few stops along the way, we arrived in Yuma, around noon on the 15th day of August 1945. The road was crowded with people waving little

American flags and lighting firecrackers and shooting off fireworks, shot guns and waving sparklers. When we got off the bus someone said, "The Japanese have surrendered. The war is over!" It is the memory of that celebration which keeps the date in my mind.

The rest of the trip to Los Angeles lasted late into the night. She kept me sitting next to her during that whole time. She was not fun to sit next to.

Once in the Los Angeles bus station, She had to get the suitcases and get tickets for San Francisco. She told me to sit down in one of the chairs near the soda fountain. She went to the soda fountain and got a Coke. I knew I was to get permission to get a drink from the water fountain if I was thirsty.

Some faceless middle-aged man sat next to me and said, "Are you alone, little girl?" I didn't bother to answer him. After what seemed a long time, he got up and moved on.

The voice over the loudspeakers, every few minutes, announced a bus "now loading" or "last announcement for" then the name of the town or city and state the bus would be heading for. Alternately the voices announced "bus now arriving from_ _ _" and mentioned the place the bus was coming from.

I was surprised to know there were that many places people could be from or want to go to.

The giant clock on the wall of the bus station had both hands pointing toward the ceiling when the voice announced "_ _ _ now loading for Bakersfield, Fresno and San Francisco."

ALCATRAZ: My Home Town

She motioned me to follow her. She was carrying the suitcases. She found the bus we were supposed to get on. We stood in line, under the long roof of the terminal. When it was our turn, the bus driver took Her suitcases and put them in the luggage compartment at the side of the bus. He handed Her tickets so She could claim the suitcases at the San Francisco station. I let Her get on ahead of me, knowing that any seat I picked would not be the right seat. She found two seats together and went in. I sat beside Her on the aisle. It was late and I was sleepy. Not long after we pulled out of the station, I was asleep.

On that trip I learned that bus station restrooms are usually messy and that if you are a little girl traveling alone, you can hang out in the women's restroom and those weird men will not bother you with stupid questions.

We arrived in San Francisco the following day at noontime. The bus pulled into the alley and then into a slot under another long shed. I could see Pop from the bus as we were getting off.

Pop waited near the front of the bus. The driver said the suitcases would be in the luggage room in a short time. They hugged each other, then he hugged me. His arms felt loving and safe. It was over quickly.

When they got the suitcases, we walked out of the front doors of the bus station onto the south side of Seventh Street. From there, we walked to Market Street to the streetcar line that traveled up

Sacramento Street toward the Children's Hospital on the west side of the city.

The streetcar was almost empty. It was much like the streetcars in Los Angeles.

We got off in front of the Children's Hospital and walked up the hill to Sacramento Street. Pop carried the suitcases up the stairs of a two story, brown-shingled house with two doors on the landing between two sets of stairs up from the sidewalk.

I could see the fire engines sitting in front of the fire department on the south side of the street. A fireman waved at us. I waved back.

Pop got the key from under the welcome mat. He unlocked the door and put the key back under the mat. He motioned Her in and then told me to follow.

"This is your Aunt Eleanor's house," he said.

We entered a long hallway. Just to the left was a large heavy dark wood sliding door. Pop slid it open and we went into the living room. It was a wonder-filled room with large oil paintings on the walls, a big round table close to the floor with books, magazines and papers on it. The table had big ball-shaped feet about the size of my knees. It was painted in high gloss light green. Over in the corner, close to the hallway wall and the front window, was a tall black piano with music on the top and an open music book just above the black and white keys.

There were several big overstuffed chairs and a long comfy couch covered with a large brightly colored scarf.

ALCATRAZ: My Home Town

Under the big round table, on a low shelf, were boxes of jigsaw puzzles.

There was a fireplace shaped fixture in the middle of the far wall. In the place where a fire would have been built, there was a gas heater which, when burning, would warm the room.

We stayed there for several hours. I got permission to walk around the block and to go across the street to see the fire engines up close.

When we left the old house on Sacramento Street, we walked down the hill and crossed the street to catch the streetcar headed toward Market Street. The trip seemed quick and there were a lot more people out and about at this time of the afternoon.

We walked from Market Street down to Seventh and then toward Mission. We made it to the train station just in time to get on an electric train that would take us over the Bay Bridge, to Berkeley, where my Uncle Donald lived with his family.

Uncle Donald's place was a two-story white house with green trim. It was on McGee Street. The numbers of the house on the large round porch post read 2432.

The door on the right was open and a long dark set of stairs took us to the second floor.

We got there just in time for dinner with Donald's family around a big dining room table. After diner, three of us younger kids, Donaldina, Charley and I were told to take care of the dishes. We did as we were told.

When the dishes were finished, all of us kids went downstairs to play in the front yard. Charley was about the same age and had friends who lived near by. We played outside until it was too dark to see.

She and Pop came downstairs and onto the front porch to tell me they were going back to San Francisco, to see Bobby and that I could not go. They said that he was in Saint Francis Hospital and children under twelve years old could not visit. They left. I did not see either of them again for a very long time.

A cot was placed at the foot of Donaldina's bed so I had a place to sleep. My clothes remained in the suitcase most of the time. Aunt Alice bought me some new underwear with drawstrings to tighten and tie each time the drawers were dropped for the bathroom business. War time had removed elastic waist bands from the market place.

Donaldina gave me a couple of her old sweaters for dressing up to go school.

When school started, the first Tuesday after Labor Day, Charley let me ride on the back of his bicycle. He showed me where the office was so I could enroll. I didn't tell them I had flunked the third grade, so they put me in the fourth grade.

When school was out, Charlie was there to help me get to his house. One Saturday, She and Pop came for me to go with them to the hospital to visit. I had to stay in the lobby while they visited. When the visit was over, Pop took us to the Mayflower Donut Shop on Market Street to eat.

He helped me order. I still remember the toasted cheese sandwich with potato chips and the chocolate milk shake.

The Mayflower was a two-story restaurant and sitting downstairs, we could see people all around and upstairs eating lunch and talking and laughing. It was a great experience.

After lunch, it was back to Berkeley on the electric train, then transfer to the streetcar, then the walk to McGee Avenue and Uncle Donald's house. They left again, soon after dropping me off.

By this time, I had learned how to fold the newspapers and to help Charley with his paper route so we could play with our friends longer. There was plenty of time after dark to do homework in the house.

There does not seem to be much outstanding in my memory about this time. My oldest cousin, Lin, was home from the Navy and had started back to college at Berkeley. He was just one more person at the dinner table.

It was the last day in October 1945 when She came to get my suitcase and me. It was a Wednesday. Aunt Alice told me to stay home from school, because She was coming to pick me up. She packed the suitcase, talked with Aunt Alice for a bit, and then we left to walk to the streetcar headed to the train and to San Francisco.

Once we arrived in the city, we boarded a streetcar and, after a time, transferred to another that took us close to Saint Francis Hospital.

This day, She motioned me to follow Her to the elevator. I got in beside Her and followed when She got out. When She stopped, it was in the hospital room where Bobby had spent many weeks. He was in that big hospital bed. The back of the bed was raised so he was sitting up. He looked so happy to see me. I know I was happy to see him!

His left leg was up on a pillow. She and Pop were talking to the nurse. Bobby and I talked about his foot. He said he had surgery on the big black mole, a long time ago. The mole was then sent to three different places to see if it was cancer. That had all taken a very long time.

Because Grandfather Ziba Henry was a doctor, the surgeons wanted to be very sure they got the right diagnosis.

I was allowed to visit today because Bobby was being discharged from the hospital.

Bobby was told to get dressed. He needed help getting his left leg into his underwear and into his jeans. The nurse carefully put his left sock on before helping him with his left shoe. The left shoe was not tied tightly.

The nurse went to find a pair of crutches for Bobby. He had not been allowed to walk for a long time and would need crutches until his left leg got stronger.

ALCATRAZ: My Home Town

He walked around the room with the crutches. The nurse reminded him to put his weight on his hands, on the handles of the crutches. The nurse adjusted the height of the crutches several times.

Grandfather Henry told us he would drive us to the dock. Neither Bobby nor I knew what he was talking about.

When we got out the front door of the hospital, we waited until Grandfather drove up to the curb, then Pop told each of us where to sit in the big dark car with big seats and comfortable cushions.

I got into the back seat first and scooted to the far side by the door. Bobby got in next to me and She got in next to Bobby. Pop sat in the front seat with Grandfather.

The ride to Pier Four was amazing and wonderful. Up and down hills over streets filled with cars, stopping now and then for red lights. It was all so neat.

ALCATRAZ HALLOWEEN PARTY

Grandfather Henry had driven us to Pier 4 from the hospital. He didn't want Bobby trying to get on and off streetcars with his crutches and the still sore, surgical site.

The MP at the guard house allowed him to drive right onto the pier, where he turned the car around before telling us we could get out and wait for the boat, which should be arriving soon. Pop got out of the front seat and opened the right-hand passenger door for Her.

I opened the car door on my side and slid out to hold the door for Bobby. He slid out and placed his crutches to help him stand and walk. We went to the east side of the dock to see the water under the Municipal Pier and watch it flap gently against the concrete of the piers. Nowhere in Arizona could we have ever seen this much water.

The sun was shining and it felt good to be outside. This was the first time for the adventure of taking the boat to Alcatraz. Neither Bobby nor I knew that this would become a part of our everyday lives.

ALCATRAZ: My Home Town

My father had arranged for us to go to the island on the afternoon launch. We arrived at Pier 4 in time to see the Warden Johnston round the east corner of Alcatraz as it made the ten-minute trip to the mainland, at the foot of Van Ness Avenue, on the Fort Mason dock.

My first home on Alcatraz was the old Army chapel.

The sun shone on Alcatraz Island, in the middle of the bay. It looked beautiful and peaceful, belying a history of violence, which preceded the presence of the "world's toughest prison."

The north side of the island displayed the threatening look of the prison with the high dock tower, the visible correctional officer carrying a rifle, the large sign warning boats to stay well away from the place and the old Spanish prison building reeking of history.

We disembarked onto the little floating dock, walked up the concrete stairs across to the metal detector and into the dock office where we were signed in as "visitors". Then Pop led the way up the hill to the tunnel, up an inside stairwell to the road above and up another set of steps into the place he called home. He lived there with my two older brothers, Harold and Bill.

Harold and Bill were Pops' children from his first marriage. Their mother, Helen, had died when Bill was four years old. Irene became their stepmother when Pop married Her in 1934. They did not like Her at all and had arranged to be away from Alcatraz when they heard She was coming to visit.

Although I didn't know it at the time, the building Pop lived in had been the chapel for the members of the armed services before the Federal Bureau of Prisons took over the Island.

The front doors were fixed so that only the right side opened. Once inside, the ceilings were high and curved to a peak. The windows were about eight feet up the wall on three sides of the building, letting in a lot of light. The floors were of a light colored hardwood and the big church had been cut in thirds. One third was living room, one third was a bedroom with three single beds placed against different walls and the last third was a kitchen area with an electric stove and a small refrigerator with a table and chairs against the north wall.

Pop fixed dinner for the three of us about five in the afternoon. As trained, Bobby and I ate what was put on our plates. I don't remember what he had cooked, I was just impressed that he would cook.

She was close to him the whole time, touching his arm or, at the dinner table, rubbing the top of his leg with her hand.

When the dishes were done, Bobby was told to go lay down on the couch in the living room and put his leg up on a pillow. They found a radio program for him to listen to.

Pop said I should go to the Halloween Party. As a farm kid, I had no idea what "Halloween" was, much less what a party would be like. He explained that the kids would dress up in funny clothes and get to play games and get candy to eat. He said "You'll have a lot of fun and you'll get to meet kids your own age."

He found a pair of his old boxer shorts and an undershirt for me to put on over the clothes I was wearing. It felt funny, but it wasn't the first time in my life I had felt odd in my clothes, so I co-operated.

He walked me down the road to the west of his place. The Social Hall was brightly lit and happy noises were coming from inside the double doors. He told me to walk inside and to stay until the party was over. It was a time when children did not question adults.

Inside there were more children of different sizes than I had ever seen anywhere except school. Each was dressed in a costume to look like a fairy tale character or a comic book character or someone other than a child. There were princesses, pirates, cowboys and cowgirls, clowns, fat ladies with pillow bellies and beasts and ghosts, among other fantasy characters, the likes of which I had never seen.

The activities, as I remember, included a dark room where all of us children sat around a table. As the story was told about a post mortem exam, parts taken from the human body were passed around the table, from hand to hand. I could feel, but could not see, the eyeballs (two grapes), the guts (cooked cold spaghetti), the tongue (two inches off the tip of a leather belt), a finger bone (wing bone of chicken) and on until the story teller jumped up and screamed something scary to frighten all the children and suddenly the lights went on.

In the main area of the Social Hall there were games set up for the children to enjoy. There was a big galvanized tub filled with water for apple bobbing, which required kneeling on the floor beside the tub with your hands behind your back while you grabbed a floating apple with your teeth and bite it firmly enough to lift it out of the water.

Near a wall was a big cardboard frame with balloons blown full of air, tied to thumbtacks with ribbon. The player was given five darts and was given a point for each balloon popped with the thrown dart. The thrower was then allowed to pick a prize for points earned. Prizes included wrapped bubble gum, several Tootsie Pops, a bubble pipe or a box of candy cigarettes.

After what seemed a rather long time, a man with a microphone asked the children to arrange themselves in groups according to age. The pre-school children were in the first group. When instructed, the little children were led around in a circle as the mother or father held the child's' hand. After they had marched around in time to the martial music, a judge picked a first, a second, and a third-place winner for best costume. The prizes were colored ribbons.

After the little kids, it was time for the six to nine-year-old kids to walk around in a circle in time to the music. The process was the same. The best three costumes were picked and the three winners were awarded colored ribbons. I was in no danger of winning. A couple of the kids asked me who I was. When I told them, they still didn't know, but at least we had talked.

There were several other age groups judged before it was time for all the children to go home. The man with the microphone asked the kids not to go "Trick-or-treating" because many of the officers were sleeping at this time because they had to work the night shift.

As the children left the main hall, a man handed each child a small brown paper bag of Halloween candy. We all walked up the hill toward the gate. As I turned to the left to go up the steps to the house where Pop lived, some of the other kids waved good night. It felt good to wave back. I opened the big door and was surprised that it opened to let me in.

Bobby had been dozing on the couch, but he woke up in time to share the candy in the brown bag. He and I talked about the party. He was sorry that he had missed it and was glad to eat candy with me.

He and I both "smoked" a candy cigarette, then called it a night by undressing down to our underwear and going to bed for our first night on Alcatraz.

As I was drifting off to sleep, I became aware of a new noise. Off in the distance was the soft sound of tin cups being rubbed back and forth over metal bars. The sound was mournful. After a time, I learned that the sound came from the cell blocks, in the prison, where the inmates would mark every special holiday with the sound of tin cups running over the metal bars of their cells.

When morning came, She and Pop had been up for awhile, in the kitchen, drinking coffee and smoking as they talked. I woke Bobby. He and I got dressed before going into the kitchen.

The bathroom was at the far end of the kitchen. We had to pass by the chair Pop was sitting in to get to it. Bobby got to go first. He had a difficult time using the crutches to move sideways along the narrow space between Pops' chair and the wall.

Pop made hot cereal for breakfast. When breakfast was over, She and Pop talked to us about what was going to happen on this day. It had been decided that She was taking the Greyhound bus back to Douglas this afternoon. I was to stay on Alcatraz with Pop. Bobby, She had decided, would be allowed to return to Douglas with her only if he could learn to walk without crutches. She told him She did not want to be bothered with his crutches. Bobby started to cry softly.

"Can we go up to the Parade Ground?" I asked.

"Sure" said Pop, "Here, take this key so you can unlock the lock on the gate."

Bobby and I walked down the front steps of the big house where Pop lived, then across the lower road to the three steps leading to the upper road and up to the Little Parade Ground. The officer in the dock tower waved at us. We waved back. Then slowly, ever so slowly, we walked up to the gate, where I unlocked the lock, lifted the handle and opened the gate to let Bobby in with his crutches. Then I closed the gate and locked the handle in place.

On the Parade Ground I explained to Bobby that he needed to learn to walk without the crutches if he wanted to go home with Her on the Greyhound Bus.

At first, he walked with the crutches, but put less and less weight on the handles of the crutches and more and more weight on his left foot. The leather had been cut away from the top of the left shoe, over the two little toes of the surgery site. That kept the shoe from hurting that area.

It seemed like a very long time, but finally, he was able to walk without the crutches. We sat on the steps of the Little Parade Ground for a while to rest.

I carried his crutches so he could practice walking without them. I unlocked the gate and let him go through before I locked the gate behind us. The downhill slant was a new challenge for him, but he did it. He took the three steps down, walked across the road and up the stairs to Pops' door. I opened the door for him and he walked in without his crutches.

"Look at Bobby," I said, "he can walk without his crutches."

Bobby walked into the room and walked around the living room and looked so proud. This was a big accomplishment!

Pop told Bobby he was very proud of him for learning to walk without the crutches. Bobby smiled and his eyes twinkled.

"Too bad," She said, "you still can't go with me. I don't want you on the bus."

She and Pop left on the noon boat so he could get her to the bus station and off to Arizona.

Bobby and I stayed in Pops' place. Bobby cried off and on all afternoon. I was so happy to be away from Her. I did not understand why Bobby was so upset at being left by Her and I never would.

DAY TWO ON ALCATRAZ

To fully appreciate the following story, you will need some background information.

Once, in 1942, my brother and I were at a Ringling Brothers Circus with my mother and stepfather. We were offered a choice between a big red balloon and pink cotton candy on a stick. The three-ring circus was over and we were on our way to the parking lot with the grownups before we finally chose the cotton candy.

Buyers' remorse set in, as soon as we finished the cotton candy.

World War II was in full flare and the nightly news, "brought to you by Life Buoy soap" and the fog horn sound, were the last sounds we heard as we drifted off to sleep, in the old adobe farm house outside the town of Douglas, Arizona. Rubber was scarce, as it was a war material. Balloons were even more scarce.

During the summer days, my brother and I were left alone on my stepfather's poultry farm. On Tuesdays and Thursdays, Juan, the hired hand, would come early in the morning. We would join him in his slaughterhouse to work.

We would help him catch the number of live chickens he had been told to slaughter of the market that day. Each was placed, with others in a small cage outside the slaughterhouse. Juan took each, one at a time, turned it head down and placed the bird in a funnel shaped cone with its head sticking out the bottom. He used a pliers with a cutting edge, to cut the roof of the chicken's beak, so the bird would bleed to death.

When dead, each chicken was dipped into a big pot of hot water to make plucking easier. We helped pluck the chickens. Then it was time to clean out the innards. Gizzard, liver and heart were stuck back into the body cavity. Then Juan would help us find the chicken bladder.

The first time, Juan did it so we could see each step of the process. Then he watched as I did it all by myself in the following manner. Checking through the chicken guts, I found the chicken bladder. Using a carving knife, I cut the intestinal tube that ran into the bladder. Then I cut the tube leading out of the bladder. Once the bladder was freed, I tied a knot in the exit tube. Then while stretching the entry tube over my lips, I blew as hard as I could until the chicken bladder filled with air. The chicken bladder would grow to the size of Juan's fist, sometimes even bigger!

The air-filled chicken bladder became a lightweight, translucent ball to bounce around in the air or play catch with. Great fun! With this recall, the mucus feel over my lips comes back.

My next adventure with balloons came several years later. The date was November 2, 1945. My mother had left us with my father on Alcatraz Island. He worked there as a correctional officer.

We had been in my father's home only a few days. He was not at home when we woke up. We decided he must be at work. We had not yet been enrolled in school, although it was a regular school day for the other Alcatraz children.

Alone in this big, new place, Bobby and I just had to explore. In my father's room on his chest of drawers was a beautiful black box. When I lifted the lid, the inside top was covered with silky, shiny fabric while the bottom inside was black velvet slots, which seemed to be separated with small, shiny silver packages. I tore open one of the tinfoil wrapped packages and found a round, thin, slippery pale material, which felt like a chicken bladder.

"Balloons!" I said. I blew one up as big as it would go. It was as long as my forearm and as big around as my wrist. I had never seen a chicken bladder balloon that big! It was wonderful!

Bobby and I played with the balloon for a while. Then we had a great idea. We could take the balloons up to the parade ground and sell them; the way the man was selling them at the circus.

ALCATRAZ: My Home Town

We blew up three balloons and tied off the ends. Then we found our gate key and walked up the hill to the gate leading into the little parade ground.

The officer in the dock tower waved at us. We waved back.

The little parade ground was empty. Not a soul.

We walked over to the big parade ground. Nobody was there, either. We went over to the other side of the handball building, to the sand box and the swings. We played in the swings for a time, holding the balloons away from the chains and taking special care against the wind.

We were about to give up selling the balloons, when a tall man wearing the charcoal prison uniform approached us. He said, "Are you the Henry kids?"

"Yes sir." I said. It felt good to be in a place were somebody knew our family name.

He said, "Just spoke with your dad. He'd like you to get home as soon as you can. What are you doing with those things?"

"We're going to sell them to the kids for two cents a piece."

"Not today," he responded.

My brother was still limping from a recent foot surgery, but we walked as fast as we could, back across the little parade ground, to the locked gate, which I unlocked. We went through the gate and locked it behind us, then down the hill and up the stairs into my father's apartment.

He was waiting for us in the living room. He appeared taller that morning, than I remembered him from the night before.

"What are you doing with those?" he asked without waiting for a response. His voice was very moderated and patient as he said, "Those are my things and you did not ask permission to be in my private space."

"We are going to live here together," he continued. "We must trust one another. You have a right to your private space and I will not go into that space. I have a right to private space and you will not go into my private space. Do we have an understanding?"

"Yes Sir." And that was the end of my entrepreneurial spirit, at least for a time.

MORE FAMILY

On the first weekend of November, my brother Harold came home from the city, where he had been staying to avoid contact with Her.

At that time, the only phone between Alcatraz and the outside world was in the prison armory. There was no convenient way for him to know the activities of the household.

When Harold got home on the ten o'clock boat, Bobby and I were listening to "Let's Pretend", a Saturday morning radio program.

He told us to get dressed and get ready to go to town on the noon boat. "Your sister, Dottie, is going to want to see you both," he said. "She hasn't seen you since you were diaper babies."

Neither Bobby nor I remembered other brothers or sisters. We had so much to learn about our family.

Harold walked us down to the dock, through the dock office and, when the boat horn tooted, onto the Warden Johnston. He asked us if we wanted to sit outside on the back of the boat. We were thrilled.

ALCATRAZ: My Home Town

The trip over the bay to the bottom of Van Ness Avenue was still exciting for us.

Within ten minutes, we were at Pier 4.

Bobby and I were the only kids on the boat, so we got to go next and Harold was right behind us as we stepped off the boat and onto the moving gangplank and up the ramp to the concrete of the dock.

We walked up the dock to the military police shack, at the base of Fort Mason and then up the hill to the corner of Van Ness Avenue and Bay Street, where we caught a streetcar headed toward Market Street. Harold sat outside with us, so we could have the thrill of the ride and see the sights of the big city.

Everything was new to us. Blocks of tall apartment buildings, interspersed with corner drug stores and little coffee shops, then the new car dealerships with the big glass encased showrooms and the San Francisco Opera House, pointed out by Harold, who loved classical music.

Soon, we had crossed Market Street and it was time to get off the streetcar. We hopped onto a different streetcar, which would take us further down Mission. We got off that streetcar at 22nd Street.

The three of us walked west on 22nd two very long blocks to Dolores Street, where we turned left and walked to a three story flat in the middle of the block. We went up the wide wooden stairs to a landing fronted by two doors. Harold knocked on the door on the left and waited.

My sister Dottie

The dark haired young woman who answered the door obviously knew Harold. Her skin was darker than his, but they both had the same black hair. Her eyes darted from him to Bobby and then to me. "Oh my God!" she said.

She stooped to hug us both and welcomed us into her apartment. "This is your sister, Dottie," Harold said, smiling.

As she moved things, to make room for us to sit down, she talked about the last time she had seen us. According to her, I was two years old when she and Harold and Bill were put on a Greyhound bus, in Douglas, Arizona and sent to San Francisco.

None of the conversation about the last time she saw us, made any sense. I could not remember anything about that time or the people in my life then.

It was afternoon and we were hungry. Dottie made lunch for all of us. As we ate, she and Harold caught up on recent events about how Bobby and I had been left on Alcatraz for Pop to take care of.

Soon after we ate, there was the cry of a little baby coming from another room. As Dottie went to get the baby, Harold explained that our sister, Dottie, was married to a soldier who was serving in the war. He would be coming home soon, Harold said, because the war was over.

Dottie brought Gail, her baby, into the living room. Fascinated by the baby, I asked if I could hold her. She fit well into my arms and I was allowed to hold the bottle for her as she sucked it dry.

Later in the day, we went across the street to another flat, where one of my sister's friends lived with her mother.

The friend's mother, Edna, invited Bobby and me to go to church with her. She had to go to confession in order to be able to accept the sacraments on Sunday.

Bobby was tired out from walking so much, but I was willing to walk with her and to see more of the big city up close.

Edna and I walked the five blocks to Mission Dolores. City blocks were really long. Almost a block away from the mission, the cross on the top of the two-story building could be seen.

Though I did not know it at the time, Mission Dolores was the oldest intact building in San Francisco. The early Spanish settlers had built it in 1776.

We walked up the front steps, through the heavy front doors, and into the front lobby. On each side of the opening into the main church, were washbasin-sized sculptures for holy water.

Edna dipped her fingertips into the water, and then touched her forehead, her lower middle chest, her left chest, and then her right chest. Following her lead, I did the same.

Then I followed her into the main church, across the back of the room and up toward the middle, across from two closet-sized curtained booths. She motioned for me to sit in the pew. After I had sat down, she knelt beside the pew, and then followed me. She did not sit. She knelt on a little knee rest and seemed to pray.

ALCATRAZ: My Home Town

While she was doing that, I looked around. What a beautiful place. There were life-like statues of Biblical characters, evenly spaced, all around the walls. Though it took me a long time, I finally figured out that the statues told the story of the crucifixion of Jesus.

Near the front of the church was a beautiful, dark wood railing, with a kneeling rail directly in front of it. An opening in the middle had carpeted steps up to an altar with more crosses and more artwork. The sight kept my eyes busy for a long time.

Someone came out of one of the little closets. Edna got up from her kneeling position and walked to the closet, went in and pulled the curtain closed behind her. She stayed there for several minutes.

When Edna came out, she motioned to me to follow her. We walked up to the front of the church where there were hundreds of little candles burning in little red glasses. Edna put some change into the slot on the front of the metal rack, then lit one of the candles and prayed quietly for several minutes.

When she finished, we walked to the back of the church, where she knelt again, and then out the same door we had come in through.

Every time we went into that church, I got the feeling that statues could see through the wooden pews, so even if I itched anywhere near my panties, I wouldn't scratch.

In the evening, at Edna's place, she asked Harold questions about my father and his many children.

Harold explained, "Paul and Alice are the children of Helen and a Mexican man.

"Helen was Navajo Indian and met my father soon after WWI, near Douglas, Arizona. They got married and lived on a large horse ranch with many of the people from Helen's tribe. While there, Pop learned a lot about horses, including how to deliver colts if the mare was having a difficult birth.

"Helen had three children with my father. At that time, most babies were born at home. Pop assisted Helen in giving birth to Dottie, Harold Junior and Bill.

"When Bill was four years old, Helen got tuberculosis. The hospital in Douglas would not allow Indians to be treated there, so she had to go to the reservation for treatment. She died that year and was buried on the Navajo Reservation.

"My father left the horse ranch and moved into a two-story house in Douglas, where he worked as a newspaper reporter for the Douglas Dispatch. Pop hired a young Mexican woman to clean the house and cook three meals a day, and another woman to care for the children.

"While working at the Dispatch, Pop met Irene, who was a senior in high school. She had roller-skated to the Douglas Dispatch to put an ad in the paper. He was 35 years old. She was almost 17.

"He and Irene were married. Because he had delivered his other children at home, he was surprised when she insisted on having her babies in the hospital.

ALCATRAZ: My Home Town

"Bobby was born in December of 1934. Baby was born in May of 1936. Baby's given name is Haroldene, because Pop thought girls should be named after their fathers, too."

It was late when Harold finished giving Edna information about our family. Bobby had already fallen asleep. Edna said we should spend the night and have breakfast in the morning before going back to the Island. Everyone agreed, it had been a long busy day.

On Sunday morning we had hot chocolate and toast for breakfast. Edna left for church. We crossed the street to say bye to Dottie, then Harold took Bobby and me on the walk to Mission Street to catch the street car headed back to Market Street and a transfer to another car headed north on Van Ness Avenue.

We got to the dock and waited for the "Warden Johnston", the Alcatraz boat, to arrive with people headed for church. After they all got off, we were able to get right on. We were the only people on the boat that morning.

Back at Pop's apartment, Harold showed us where the house-cleaning equipment was kept and explained how he expected us to help keep the place neat and clean.

While we were cleaning, he played music on his phonograph. His collection took up a shelf about three feet long. I could tell he took excellent care of his collection. Harold fixed lunch for us and we all sat together to eat.

After lunch, Bobby and I listened to the radio dramatic programs, including "The Barber Family", a story of a wealthy San Francisco family, who lived in the hills overlooking the Pacific Ocean.

Harold went to visit his Island friends, while Bobby and I sat looking through the Sunday funnies and the magazines on the coffee table.

It was late afternoon when Pop got home from work. He seemed happy to see us and asked about our weekend adventures.

When Harold got home, he and Pop made dinner. Steak, canned green beans, canned corn and baked potatoes were likely the meal, as that was what was easiest for Pop to fix.

During the dinner conversation Harold said he would be leaving for the Navy on Wednesday, as he had volunteered for the service. He and Pop had a conversation about why Navy and not Army. "Grandpa is an Army man", Pop explained.

It was near the end of dinner that Pop asked Harold to take me to San Francisco and get me enrolled in school on Monday morning. I had no great longing to be in school. I had already missed much of the semester because of the travel from Douglas to Berkeley and then to San Francisco and Alcatraz.

Bobby had to get grandfather Henry to sign something before he could go to school. Pop told us

ALCATRAZ: My Home Town

that his days off would be Tuesday and Wednesday for the next three months. Because he would be off on Tuesday, he said, he would take Bobby to Grandpa's and get the written permission for him to go to school. "I'll get him enrolled in school right after we get through at Grandpa's."

After dinner, Harold washed the dishes, I dried them and Bobby put them away. Pop went into the living room and sat in the big blue easy chair near the standing lamp, put his feet up on the ottoman and read the San Francisco News. While he was reading, the radio was tuned to an evening news program with Walter Winchell.

That evening, when it was time for bed, Bobby and I slept in the beds Harold and Bill usually slept in and Harold slept on the couch in the living room. Bill hadn't come home yet and no one seemed upset.

Monday morning Pop had left for work when Bobby and I got up to have breakfast with Harold.

As was my habit, I had gotten dressed for the day soon after I woke. There were only two dresses in the suitcase She had left us with. None of the clothing had been unpacked. Neither dress was ironed, but both were clean. There were two pairs of panties. One pair I was wearing; the other pair was dirty. My shoes were brown tie shoes with white socks.

Harold reminded me to brush my hair before he and I left the apartment to walk down to the dock for the 8:20 boat. The dock was crowded with kids going to school. Some of them looked familiar from the Halloween Party.

The boat officer sounded the all aboard whistle, one short toot. A small group of women moved across the dock, down the gangplank and onto the boat, followed by the children, then the men, some of whom had worked all night.

My big brother kept me close to him. He introduced me to some of his high school friends. We sat outside on the back of the boat. He talked with them about signing up for the Navy. His friend, Jim, had signed up at the same time. They would be going to San Diego together.

At Pier 4 we walked with his friends until about half way up the Van Ness Avenue hill. He and Jim stopped by an old black model "A" Ford. Jim twisted opened the handle on the back of the car and pulled. Out popped a rumble seat. He and Harold helped me climb in and sit down, and then they flipped a coin to see who would drive.

The old car drove up Van Ness Avenue to Green Street where we turned right and went over two blocks to Gough Street, made another right turn and parked across from Sherman Elementary School.

Harold took my hand and led me in through the front door, down the hall to the office. We went inside where he spoke to a secretary. She smiled at me. He filled out some papers, then handed me a bunch of papers and said, "Take these home to Pop this afternoon."

ALCATRAZ: My Home Town

Harold hugged me goodbye and left me with the lady from the office.

She took me to the end of the hall and up the stairs to the second floor. She had me follow her to a door on the south side of the hall. She knocked gently on the door and waited for the teacher to come. The teacher was a short, white haired lady, dressed in a one-piece, dark blue dress with no frills. She talked quietly to the secretary for a few minutes, and then she said, in a friendly voice, "Welcome, Haroldene." She motioned me to follow her into the classroom where she introduced me to the class before finding me a desk near the back of the classroom. At that time in my life, I was tall for my age and often had to sit in the back.

Before the day was over, she gave me three hard covered books and told me I needed to take them home and cover them. She promised that she would check on the books the next day.

The dock tower where the officer carries a gun while
overlooking the second balcony of the
#64 building, the north-and east-bay area

ALCATRAZ: My Home Town

School was out around 3 o'clock in the afternoon. One of the kids in my class was Shirley Kelly. She was one of a set of twins and her dad worked on Alcatraz too. She said she would walk with me to the dock. She and I walked and talked all the way to the dock. We made good time and joined other Alcatraz kids on the dock to wait for the 3:30 boat.

We got on the boat and sat down in the cabin together on one of the wide seats with the other children. When we landed at the Alcatraz dock, we got off and went through the metal detector in single file. Shirley told me she would see me in the morning, and she ran up the long concrete stairs to the first balcony of #64 Building. The officer in the dock tower watched and when the children got close enough, he unlocked the electric gate to let them inside the fence.

I walked up the sidewalk toward the tunnel, then up the stairs to the road above and around to the stairs up to Pops' apartment. Bobby met me at the door. He was walking better and seemed really happy to have company. We talked about Sherman School and some of the kids I had met on the boat coming home.

By the time Pop got home, Harold had come home from the city. We all helped set the table and got dinner ready. At the dinner table Pop said, "Warden Johnston (the man in charge of the prison) wants us to move inside the fence. He doesn't want kids, especially girls, outside the fence. We're going to move tomorrow. Harold and I will move all of the household stuff and when you get home tomorrow afternoon, I'll take you both up to the new place, inside the fence."

So, it was on that Tuesday, after getting Bobby started at Sherman School, Pop and Harold moved all the personal belongings from the big apartment outside the fence, to the little white cottage up on the big parade ground.

Pop was waiting for us when Bobby and I got home from school. It was almost 4 o'clock when he walked us up the hill, through the gate to the little parade ground, along the sidewalk and to the little white cottage with the windbreak porch.

This would be our new home.

THE LITTLE WHITE COTTAGE DAYS

The porch was crowded with the three of us there. Pop opened the door into a large bedroom. The double bed was on the north side of the room with a four-drawer dresser separating the head of the bed from the little single bed on the south side of the room, where I would sleep. There was a makeshift closet, made of plywood standing upright at the foot of the single bed. A wood rod for clothes hangers was set in the center and a cotton drape covered the opening.

We walked around the corner into the living room where Pop's easy chair sat in front of the ottoman. The room looked comfortable with an overstuffed couch and Pop's chair. Windows on the north wall looked out over the North Bay area. The big window on the south wall revealed the big parade ground with the new apartment buildings, the sandbox and gymnasium, on the right. The big blue-white two-story duplex, where the associate warden and the minister lived with their families, was on the left.

ALCATRAZ: My Home Town

My brother Harold had set up his phonograph with his record collection along the far wall of the living room, near the north window.

The dining table sat in front of the south window. Four maple chairs were in their places near the table.

The kitchen was crammed into a little space on the southwest side of the cottage. It contained a refrigerator, an electric four-burner stove with an oven, and a sink and side boards on the west wall. The cupboards were boards hung at the appropriate height above the sink and stove. This little cottage became my wonderful new home.

Pop had us sit down for milk and cookies while he questioned us about our day at school. He encouraged us to do any homework that might have been assigned. Bobby had to get brown paper bag covers on the schoolbooks that had been sent home with him.

My brother, Harold came in about five o'clock. He and Pop got dinner on the table. Bobby and I set the table for dinner. The dinner was the usual, steak, canned green beans, canned corn, and a baked potato. Salt, pepper and sugar were on the table. The yellow stuff we put on the potatoes was not butter.

A routine began that, after dinner, Bobby and I would take turns washing or drying the dishes and putting them away. Harold went out after dinner to visit friends. This would be his last night on the Island before reporting for duty with the Navy in San

Diego. He would be sleeping on the couch this evening.

Pop would be off work on Wednesday morning, so he was there to see us off to school after breakfast. Harold hugged us goodbye as we left the cottage to go to the 8:20 boat, for school.

As we walked along the first balcony, the other kids began to look familiar. Shirley and Sandy were just coming out of the door to their apartment as we walked by. I introduced them to Bobby. Several of the women, who lived along this balcony, had come out to visit with each other and to see the children get on the boat.

Things were becoming more familiar. The race up the hill between the public school kids and the Catholic school kids in their uniforms was fun.

Vaughn Scandland, a non-competitive kid, walked with my brother. The walks to and from school were the best part of the day. There were several recesses during the school day. The mid day recess was for lunch. Groups of friends would join in games or just stand around and chat.

After school, most of the Alcatraz kids would walk in a loose knit group down to Pier 4. That gave us all a chance to get to know each other better.

Everything was going well, until mid-morning on Saturday. I was listening to the Saturday morning kids radio programs and drawing pictures.

Bobby decided to go out on the big parade ground to meet a group of boys who attended Catholic school. I could see him, through the big window by the dining table. After almost half an hour, he came back to the cottage and asked me to go outside with him. "They want to meet you," he said.

I was wearing my "farm kid" coveralls when I left the cottage with my brother, to meet the new kids.

They were standing over by the gymnasium, to get out of the cool breeze. They eyed me closely as I approached.

The tall, skinny kid with black hair and blue eyes, who seemed to be the leader of the group said, "So you can beat me up?"

"If I have to," I responded. My unwritten assignment had always been to protect Bobby from the bad guys. Even though Bobby was eighteen months older than I, Grandmother Gibbons had tamed most of the boy out of him.

Someone, in the group, had threatened to beat up Bobby, he told me later, so he had told them, "Haroldene can beat up all of you."

"I'm not supposed to hit girls," said Donny Hurley, the gang leader.

That was the beginning of a long tentative friendship for all of us. The boys introduced themselves as Donny Martin, Bobby Orr, both short for their age and Donny Hurley.

The five of us had a great morning playing in the sandbox, standing doubles, swinging high, trying to swing over the bar, then running up and down the see-saw without falling. We competed, placing one foot in front of the other, walking the thin board framing the sand box from one side of the building to the other. It was a great morning for all of us.

Around noon, everybody went home for lunch. Bobby and I found the peanut butter and jelly for sandwiches.

Don Hurley, who threatened my brother Bobby.

The milk was in the refrigerator in quart-sized bottles. On the farm, our milk had been stored in gallon glass jars. The Alcatraz inmates, supervised by an officer, delivered milk on Mondays, Wednesdays and Fridays,

Pop got home in the late afternoon. He picked up the newspaper that had been delivered by Larry, an older teenaged newspaper boy. After greeting us, Pop sat down, lit a Lucky Strike cigarette, and began to read the paper.

Bobby and I went outside. We walked east on the sidewalk toward the rusted iron gate in the rock wall around the parade ground, leading to a lookout point bench and a path down to the beach.

Just before we got to the gate, a girls' voice called out, "You can't go out there until you're sixteen years old." The girl was Betty Lou Orr, Bobby Joe's sister. She had been shopping in San Francisco with her mother and had come home on the noon boat. Bobby Joe had told her about our morning together. It was time for us to get to know each other.

She had dark curly hair and was my size and just one year older. (In fact, her birthday was one day before mine, in May.) She was one of the kids who attended Catholic School.

Her mother had some sort of office job in San Francisco, so she was part of the group known as "working women". Betty Lou and Bobby were expected to take care of themselves on the days their mom worked in the city and their dad worked as a correctional officer. They were also expected to clean up the house every afternoon, when they got home from school and to start dinner about five in the afternoon so the family could eat when the mother returned home from work on the five o'clock boat.

Bob Orr. His mother was a "working woman."
Little White Cottage on far left behind him

Betty told us she couldn't be out very long but asked if we could go to church with her on Sunday morning. It would be several months before I went with her to church. It was good to know that she, even being Catholic, was not very different from other girls I had met. She was a bit of a tomboy, too.

Sunday stands out only because that is the day that Pop would come home and say, "Change the sheets on the beds and make them up. We need to make the laundry list."

Once the beds were remade, he would sit down with the dirty laundry bag and dump everything out on the living room floor. He would sit in his big chair and have Bobby and me pick out dirty clothes, item by item. As we counted and named the item, Pop would check it on the laundry list. "Fifteen pairs of sox, seven pair of men's shorts, six pair of girl's panties, five bath towels," and on and on.

When we were through with the list, all the dirty clothes were in the laundry bag, which would be left on the porch Monday morning for the inmate crew to pick up and take to the laundry. Later in the week, a bundle of clean clothes, wrapped in plain brown paper, would be left on the porch with the laundry bag, washed and neatly folded at the bottom of the stack.

In no time at all, Bobby and I had found a home with Pop, on Alcatraz. She was not present here.

I don't remember Thanksgiving the year of 1945. I do know that had I prayed, it would have been to thank God for placing Bobby and me in the care of our father, in the little cottage on Alcatraz.

SANTA CLAUS LIVES ON ALCATRAZ

Pop had taken Bobby and me to town, about two weeks before Christmas. There, in a Christmas tree lot on Van Ness Avenue, he got our first Christmas tree.

Neither Bobby nor I had ever had a Christmas tree in our very own home before. It was so exciting!

We took the Christmas tree on the streetcar first, and then Pop carried it as he walked down the long hill with us. That wonderful Christmas smell comes back to my nostrils as I write.

Back on the Island, Pop rode the bus up the hill, with the tree. Bobby and I ran up the stairs, along the balcony, up the long irregular stairs to the parade ground and along the sidewalk to our little cottage, trying to beat Pop. We won and the wait for Pop seemed eternal!

Finally, Pop got there with the tree and soon made a stand for it. We set it up in front of the window on the north side of the living room.

Pop, from some mysterious place, drug out a box of Christmas tree decorations, some of which were pre-World War I. Never had I touched Christmas ornaments. If you have always celebrated and always had a Christmas tree, it must seem difficult to imagine how special this all was for me.

Pop put the Christmas lights on the tree before turning the project over to us. He told us to decorate the tree while he fixed dinner and read the newspaper.

Bobby and I took one ornament at a time and hung it, ever so carefully, on a branch, making sure not to put more than one ornament per branch and to space them around and up and down to cover the tree well.

When we had finished, Pop got a white sheet from the bottom drawer of the dresser and covered the bottom of the tree around the floor. It looked kind of like snow.

Being off from school for the week before Christmas gave us a chance to see the trees of other Alcatraz families.

The very best tree was in Eddy Faulk's house. Faulk's tree almost touched the ceiling and the little village beneath was built on a mountainside with a toy electric train running the length of their living room. Christmas candies sat about in little bowls and the walls were also hung with Christmas decorations.

Being with the Alcatraz kids helped us get a grasp of this kind of Christmas. It was so different from what either of us was used to.

On the evening of December 24th, 1945, Pop took Bobby and me to the Social Hall where, he promised, we would meet Santa Claus.

Marvin Orr, another correctional officer, and his committee would start soon after Thanksgiving, to decorate the Social Hall. Mr. Orr was gifted with crepe paper.

The Social Hall had been decorated with green and red crepe paper twisters streaming up and down across the high ceiling and huge white paper napkin snowballs surrounding the big hanging lights. Chairs were set up for the special Christmas play featuring the birth of a baby in a manger. The cast of characters was the children of Alcatraz who had been picked by their mothers to appear in this special showing.

Mrs. McKean, Stanley's mom, had been teaching the children Christmas Carols. The children started caroling, just outside the fence, near "A" Building. Then they were herded toward "B" Building. They sang on each of the three landings, before moving on to "C" Building. After that, they walked toward the big two-story duplex on the east side of the parade ground, past all the cottages on the north side, around the old 64 building and down toward the Social Hall.

When they arrived, each sat down in one of the chairs, in front of the stage. Bobby and I joined them.

When the curtain opened, a voice over the PA read the verses in the Bible about the birth of the baby. There was the verse about the shepherds watching their flocks by night, then the one about the three wise men traveling from "afar" following the star, and at last the one about Joseph and Mary arriving in Bethlehem and finding no room at the inn. The children, none of whom spoke a word, acted out each verse. The choir, in the back of the room, sang the appropriate carol with each scene.

As the voice on the PA system quieted, the sounds of "Away in the Manger" began at the back of the room and the choir came into the room from behind us. So many of the people we saw every day were in that choir. They sang Christmas songs which had been playing on the radio for the last month. It was beautiful. One of the moms sang "O Holy Night". It was hard to picture that angelic voice from the woman who screamed at her children daily, sounding like a hog caller.

The very last song was "Santa Claus is Coming to Town" and as the singers finished, there was the ringing of sleigh bells and the sound of a deep laughing voice with "HO! HO! HO!" and Santa Claus walked into the back of the room and around to the front as we stood to see him.

A raised area with steps was placed on the floor, in front of the stage. A large wooden chair with arms was set on the top of the raised area and Santa Claus made his way up those steps and sat in the chair.

I had seen this man on billboards off and on since the war started. Usually he was holding a Coke.

Marjory Hacks' young ballet group performing in a Christmas play

The ladies club volunteers encouraged us to line up, according to height, with the shortest ones in front and we could visit with Santa Claus. For the first time ever, Bobby said he envied Bobby Joe Orr and Donny Martin, both of whom were short for their age.

I got to stand behind Shirley Kelly, the smaller Kelly twin girl. I liked her. She was in my grade at Sherman School and we often walked home from school to the dock together. She could run fast and she was smart. She didn't get to play outside much because she had to help her mom with Elmer and Omer, the twin baby boys.

The littler kids got to sit on Santa's lap. It seemed like a very long time. Each child got to sit on his knee. No one forced a frightened child to go up on the platform. We inched nearer and nearer. Finally, it was my turn.

I sat on Santa's lap. His bright blue eyes were sparkling. He had little short stubby fingers covered with ruddy freckled skin. His face was round with chubby pink cheeks above the snowy white beard and mustache. I had learned early in my life, not to trust adults, so I examined this Santa Claus with a very sharp skeptical eye.

He said "What do you want for Christmas little girl?

"Please Santa, give me a mommy who can love me."

He replied, "Not this Christmas, but some day."

When I left his lap and stepped down the steps, I was handed a brown paper bag which contained one orange, one bright red apple, a small napkin wrapped around hard filled candies and another napkin wrapped around plain hard candies and ribbon candy and nuts.

When it was time to go home, I waited outside the Social Hall for Pop. As I was standing there, Santa came out and got into the black pick up truck, which was usually parked on the dock. He got into the passenger seat and one of the correctional officers got into the driver's side and drove Santa up the hill toward the prison. The truck stopped by the lighthouse. Now I knew where I had seen that face before. Santa lived in the lighthouse!

Bill Dolby, Tom Severson, Santa, Joe Burdette

As Pop walked Bobby and me up the hill to our little white cottage, I heard the sound of tin cups, rhythmically hitting prison cell bars. I could hear the sound of cups on the bars every time I listened during Christmas Eve.

What a wonder filled Christmas! I smiled until after the New Year.

To this day, for me, Santa Claus lives in the lighthouse on Alcatraz Island. He lives close to the house where Jackie Snyder lived. He may even have been related to Ed Snyder!

EARLY 1946

It was spring and Easter was on April 14th. Schools were out for Good Friday, so we had a three-day weekend.

Bobby had turned ten years old in December, but he was young for his age. Although I was eighteen months younger, I was the mature one.

Bobby had been home sick and often cried for his mother and I could not understand why. Pop wrote to her and arranged for Bobby to go to Douglas, by bus, on Good Friday. Pop and I went to the Greyhound bus station with him. He would arrive in Douglas on the Saturday before Easter.

Our life in the little white cottage fell into a pleasant routine. Pop was very clear in his expectation that I clean up my own messes and do my share of the meal clean up and other household jobs as needed.

On one weekend day, Pop was working while I did my Saturday routine of listening to the radio programs in the morning and going out to the parade ground after lunch to play with the other kids.

ALCATRAZ: My Home Town

This Saturday, I was the only girl in the group of about nine kids. Donny Hurley suggested that we learn how to play "spin the bottle." I had never heard of that game.

He explained that we would have to go over the rock wall to a place by the foghorn so we could play.

We found a place along the rock wall that was out of view of the apartment buildings. Over the wall we went, one by one, up onto the wall, a few scoots and down on the other side. There was a place, about ten feet down the cliff side that was flat and could accommodate us sitting in a circle.

Donny explained, as he spun the bottle, "When the top of the bottle points to you, you have to take off a piece of clothing."

The bottle stopped, pointing to Bobby Joe, who took off a shoe. Then Bobby Joe spun the bottle and it pointed to someone else. Things continued this way for quite some time. It seemed to me that I was getting more turns to spin the bottle than anyone else. I was also taking off more clothes than anyone else.

I was down to my panties, when suddenly the officer making rounds of the beach area found us.

McPherson was over six feet tall and very thin. He walked straight up to where we were, grabbed me, swatted my butt a couple of times, then wrapped me in his overcoat and told the other kids to "Get the hell out of here and go home!"

Mac took me to the little white cottage, took me inside and said, "You, young lady, wait right here for your father."

It was not long before Pop came home. I was so afraid that I would be beaten or hurt in some other way.

Pop asked me to sit on the couch, near his big chair. He sat in his chair and spoke calmly, "What you were doing often leads to having babies born, who are not wanted. Do you want any babies born who are not wanted?"

"No, sir." The answer was very clear to me. I knew what it felt like to not be wanted. I had not really thought about how babies could be wanted or not wanted. He then told me to take a bath and get dressed.

As I have said before, all of the adults on Alcatraz were responsible for all of the children. This was just the kind of supervision I needed.

It was about this time I began to attend Sunday school. According to the people who kept track of things, the women of Alcatraz had always provided Sunday school for the children living on the Island.

I arrived early and was directed by Mrs. McKean, to help move the little chairs into a semi-circle near the front of the room. There were several long low tables. Each table had little chairs setting around it. On each table was a basket of crayons and a stack of paper, so the children could draw and color pictures about the Bible stories we would hear.

ALCATRAZ: My Home Town

Near the middle right side of the big room sat a little portable organ. To make sound, it was necessary to pump each of the two flat peddles with your feet, while picking out the music with fingers on the keys.

The Sunday class was familiar. Instead of separate rooms, as it had been in Douglas, each age group occupied the chairs around one of the long low tables.

The Bible story was told with minimum of reading from the Bible. The teacher read one or two important quotes from the Bible, and the rest of the story was from a Bible storybook.

Then the story was finished, each teacher passed out pictures about the story. We were directed to color the picture with the crayons from the basket in the middle of the table. After enough time had been spent at the worktables, we were encouraged to gather near the speaker's stand. The smaller children sat near the front, with the larger children behind them.

Mrs. McKean took a seat in the little chair at the organ and, being a large woman, her butt hung off the chair on all sides, making the chair disappear. She had light red hair and a very pale complexion.

Hymnbooks were passed out as we were reminded to share with the person next to us. The tall woman standing at the speaker's stand instructed us to turn to the hymn on page (whatever) and those of us who understood turned to those pages quickly. Most of the kids there had done this before.

Mrs. McKean played the hymn all the way through. The music, as I remembered it, had a great, clear beat. The tall woman up front motioned to us to sing and on the downbeat the children, who knew the hymn, sang. It took several repetitions of the chorus before I could sing the words with the music.

"On the highways, in the hedges, Jesus is everywhere." I sang with the other children. We must have done four choruses because when Sunday school was over and we had all helped clean up, the melody and chorus was running around in my head.

Pop was still at work when I walked in the door of the little cottage. Had he been there, I might have asked him about the hymn.

The view of the bay was eye-catching. Sailboats were out and the sun was reflecting off tanks at the refinery in Richmond. It was a lovely spring day.

I sat on the floor and looked at the pictures in Life Magazine. Magazines were a new part of my life. Pop subscribed to several, including Collier's, Reader's Digest and Life.

Our radio played in the background. I became aware of an urge to pee. I started to get up from the floor to go into the bathroom when I remembered the song. Oh dear! I tried to distract myself with pictures in the magazines. For what seemed like a very long time, I was doing the "Potty dance" around our small living room floor.

ALCATRAZ: My Home Town

Time for a decision, I felt, more than thought. As I was preparing to sit on the toilet, I thought to myself, "If Jesus is silly enough to have his head there, he deserves what he gets!"

THE ALCATRAZ RIOT OF 1946

It was a warm afternoon in San Francisco on that Thursday, the second of May 1946. In just twenty days I would turn ten years old.

When Sherman School let out, all of us kids from Alcatraz began to gather near the corner of Greenwich and Franklin streets for the walk to the dock, to catch the 3:35 PM boat home. We had about thirty minutes to make it to the dock. Each afternoon, to make it fun, we'd play tag or have spontaneous races or split into teams and go down different streets toward the bay.

On this day, we raced over to Van Ness Avenue, where we met up with our friends from the Catholic School. As we crossed Lombard Street, we fanned out into a single file, about an arm length apart. Although we had started crossing with the first gleam of the green light, going as we did left five or six pedestrians in the crosswalk as the light turned red. The cars could not go until we were all out of the crosswalk. We were so pleased with the power to hold up traffic.

At the next corner, on Chestnut Street, there was a drug store with a fountain. Usually, someone would go into the drug store to buy a candy bar or a pack of gum. Left over lunch money was such a treat. We knew there was never enough candy or gum to share with everyone, so if we didn't get any that day, we knew there would be another day when we might luck out.

Two blocks to Bay Street and another crosswalk with a light at the intersection where we might do the single file walk again.

Fort Mason was an active army base. The walk was all down hill from this corner. The hill was so steep that it was dangerous to try to run down. We could look out over the bay, see Alcatraz and, if it was almost time, the boat would be on its way to pier 4. The bay was beautiful and because of the weather, sailboats were moving across the water. No waves were to be seen, the bay was calm. We walked on down to the flat of North Point Street. The big Ghirardelli Chocolate factory was on the opposite corner. The factory had to close during the war because there was not enough sugar for making chocolate.

At the flat of the hill, the train tracks led into the tunnel under Fort Mason. The trains would carry wounded military personnel to the hospital at Letterman General in the Presidio.

On the east side of the street was a snack shack in the shape of an oval. They sold coffee, soda, hot dogs, hamburgers and other light refreshments to the beachgoers in the Aquatic Park.

The flat area continued another block. Those who stayed to the right could go out on the Municipal pier for fishing or looking. Our group had to check in with the MP at the Military Police shack, and then walk on down pier 4.

The General Cox, the ferryboat serving the military stationed on Angel Island, was tied up at our dock. It would not be leaving until four o'clock. It would stop at Alcatraz to pick up the finished laundry, done by the inmates as a part of their work experience. Alcatraz residents could ride that ferry on the days it was scheduled to stop at Alcatraz.

When we first got to the dock, we lined up along the fence on the docks' east side. We could rest our arms full of books on the protective railing, while we waited. The rules were very firm. Women got on the boat first, then children, then came the men. If any child pushed in front of a woman, the boat officer would hold that child by the arm, on the rocking boat dock, until all the children had boarded. It didn't take long to learn not to break the rules.

We waited a very long time, and though none of us had watches, we knew the boat was late in arriving. Soon the officers, who had arrived to go to work on the four o'clock shift, began to speculate about why the boat might be late.

ALCATRAZ: My Home Town

BOAT SCHEDULE				BOAT SCHEDULE			
EFFECTIVE OCTOBER 11, 1959							
Leaving Alcatraz				Leaving Ft. Mason			
Weekly	Saturday	Sunday	Holiday	Weekly	Saturday	Sunday	Holiday
A.M.	A.M.	A.M.	A.M.	A.M.	A.M.	A.M.	A.M.
12:10	12:10	12:10	12:10	12:25	12:25	12:25	12:25
6:40	7:05	7:05	7:05	6:55	7:20	7:20	7:20
7:20	8:10	8:10	8:10	7:35	8:25	8:25	8:25
8:10	9:00	9:00	9:00	8:25	9:15	9:15	9:15
10:00	10:00	10:00	10:00	10:15	10:15	10:15	10:15
	11:00	11:00	11:00		11:15	11:15	11:15
P.M.	P.M.	P.M.	P.M.	P.M.	P.M.	P.M.	P.M.
12:45	12:45	12:45	12:45	1:00	1:00	1:00	1:00
3:20	3:20	3:20	3:20	3:35	3:35	3:35	3:35
3:55	4:55	4:55	4:55	4:10			
4:40	5:40	5:40	5:40	4:55	5:10	5:10	5:10
5:10	7:00	7:00	7:00	5:25			
5:40	8:45	8:45	8:45	5:55	5:55	5:55	5:55
7:00	10:00	10:00	10:00	7:15	7:15	7:15	7:15
8:45	11:15	11:15	11:15	9:00	9:00	9:00	9:00
10:00				10:15	10:15	10:15	10:15
11:15				11:30	11:30	11:30	11:30
(Reverse Side Leaving Ft. Mason)				(Reverse Side Leaving Alcatraz)			

The Warden Johnston

Finally, the Warden Johnston could be seen coming around the east side of Alcatraz. About that same time, a car arrived on the dock, carrying an officer who had been called back to work. The car radio had news blaring. Mrs. Bergen and another woman stood near the car, listening to the news.

When the boat docked, nobody got off. One of the officers, who had been called back to work, told the women and children that they could not go on the boat. "Only Federal Prison Officers" the man said.

The gangplank was removed from the gate of the General Cox and the ferryboat left the dock with no Alcatraz women or children. They would not be stopping at Alcatraz today.

Soon, newsmen began to arrive with cameras and note pads. The reporters seemed excited to be in the midst of the residents. They asked the children questions and took pictures of the family members waiting anxiously for news of their loved ones and their homes.

Mrs. Bergen, a lieutenant's wife, organized the children. She told us they were having trouble on the Island and that we might not get to go home for a long time. She suggested we do our homework or play quietly until she could arrange things.

Looking toward our hometown, we could see the smoke from gunfire, up by the prison building. Now and then, the sound of gunshots could be heard faintly. It was not likely that we'd be doing homework.

ALCATRAZ: My Home Town

Soon after five o'clock, the Warden Johnston returned for more officers in uniform. By now, the high school kids from Polly and Lowell high school had arrived at the dock. There were almost fifty young people waiting and wondering about what was happening. Again, women and children were not allowed on the boat.

By this time, Herby Stites's dad had been killed. The newspapermen seemed to know something. They began to ask questions of the children. As a group, we seemed to know we needed to protect each other. We began to make it more difficult for the news guys to be intrusive.

The sun was far in the west and the night air was cooling. The gunfire looked like sparklers on the fourth of July.

Mrs. Bergen called the Red Cross. She told us a bus would come for us and take us to dinner at a cafeteria. Now, with the promise of food, we began to feel better.

Not long after, the school bus with a big red cross on it appeared on the dock. The women, who had jobs in San Francisco, had all arrived on the dock. Those who had no friends or relatives in town were loaded into the bus. Next the children, smallest first, were allowed to get into the bus. The bus waited a long time, hoping to get all the residents who were off the Island for the day.

When the bus left Pier 4 it was dark in the streets of San Francisco. The bus driver turned left on North

Point Street and continued on to the Embarcadero, then a right turn on Mission Street to the Compton Cafeteria. Because it was several hours after the usual dinner hour the only food they had to offer was onion soup. Most of us kids did not like onion soup. We crumbled crackers into our milk and ate that.

Once everyone had eaten, we were taken to a hotel on Mission Street. Given the time of night and the numbers of people to serve, the hotel could handle the group only if we could put four children in a bed and a woman in the room near by to keep an eye on the children. I don't remember who was in the bed with me. I do remember that someone wet the bed in the middle of the night and it got cold quickly.

Very early the following morning, we were taken to the Mark Hopkins Hotel dining room for breakfast. The newspaper reporters and photographers were waiting for us as we exited the dining area. The "Grey Lady" seemed to enjoy pushing us toward the newspaper reporters and photographers.

Because she was a Red Cross volunteer, she was wearing a uniform. The uniform included a white crown-like headpiece, worn on the top of her head, and a grey, long sleeved, button down the front dress. In cold weather, there was a royal blue, button at the neck, cape with a bright red shiny lining. These women, who wore this uniform, were called "Grey Ladies."

ALCATRAZ: My Home Town

The Red Cross registered us into the hotel and gave each of us a room number. For the most part, there were two or three children in each room, each with his or her own bed and one of the Alcatraz women near by, to keep an eye on us.

A Red Cross worker bought underwear for all of us, so we could bathe and change underwear. That was wonderful.

After the bath and the change of underwear, we were loaded into a Red Cross station wagon, according to the school we attended, and driven to school. We were given specific instructions about where to meet the station wagon after school.

We were still not aware of the danger that our fathers were in, nor did any of the children know of those who had been killed or wounded.

School seemed like it was just another day. Same fourth grade subject matter, same play at recess, same old fish for lunch on Friday. The kids in my fourth-grade class apparently didn't read the paper. My fourth-grade teacher didn't mention a word about Alcatraz. Come to think of it, I don't believe many teachers knew where the children in their classes lived.

When school was out that afternoon, we joined the other Alcatraz kids near the middle of the block on Franklin, between Green and Union Street.

Junior Kelly was one of the first kids there. Then his younger twin sisters, Sandra and Shirley joined him. There were seven kids in that family, two sets of twins. Sandra and Shirley were non-identical. All of them smelled of dirty diapers. Their clothing always looked soiled and wrinkled. I was friends with the shorter twin. She was a tomboy. She was also smarter than her sister.

Jeanie Morrison was an only child. She was a couple of years younger than I and was not often on the playground with the other children. Their cottage butted right up against our place. Her father was not a correctional officer. He had a specialty in industry that allowed him to run one of the industries on the Island and to do on the job teaching to inmates. I think her mother was a "stay at home mom".

Bill Dolby was ahead of me in school. He was a smart, good-looking kid. He was another kid who didn't get to play with the others in our age group. I guess his parents had bigger plans for their children.

Herbie Stites joined the group waiting for the Red Cross station wagon, as did Stanley McKean and Vaughn Scanland.

There were several others, whose names and faces I have forgotten.

The Red Cross van finally showed up. We filed in, youngest kids first, and found seats. The driver waited to see if others would join us. When she thought all the Alcatraz kids were on board, she drove up to the corner and turned left onto Green Street and headed toward the Civic Center and the Mark Hopkins Hotel.

ALCATRAZ: My Home Town

The Red Cross van driver was a woman. Because she was a Red Cross volunteer, she was wearing a uniform.

As the kids got out of the station wagon, the press photographers were there, shooting pictures. We followed the Grey Lady into the main door of the hotel and the lobby. The Grey Lady encouraged us to sit in the center of the lobby area, at the base of the central stairway.

Members of the press began asking us questions. Questions were asked about "...the Miller children" or "the Stites children." I had no idea why, but somehow felt we were being taken advantage of and felt the need to protect our own. We formed ranks against the press and tried to ignore their questions or bump the camera man so his picture would be blurred or put a hand up in front of the lens to block the shot.

The Red Cross workers tried to get us to sit for a group picture with the tall kids standing behind the long couch and some kids sitting on the couch, with others on their knees in front of the couch. Many of the kids cooperated. Some of us made faces at the cameras.

We did not know where the Miller kids were. They were not allowed to play with most of us, even though they were in our age group. Just in case they were in the same hotel, we did not want them to learn of the death of their father from some newspaper person. We told the members of the press that the Miller who was killed was the Associate Warden.

When they started with the Stites family, we just began to treat the press like they were the enemy.

The Red Cross did nothing to protect us from the press.

Herbie's dad, Harold Stites had been killed on Thursday evening and the members of the San Francisco press knew. The kids surrounded Herb and James and would not let the press question them. We continued to protect them until we all got to go home.

When the Alcatraz women, who had jobs in town, returned to the hotel, arrangements were made for us to eat in the dining room of the hotel. Most of us had never been in a hotel dining room. One of the women was at each table to help kids pick from the menu food suitable for dinner, like macaroni and cheese.

After dinner, several groups of kids were accompanied to local movie theaters to see movies selected by the mothers in the group. Members of the Alcatraz Women's Club seemed comfortable taking the children of their friends along with their own children. As a kid without a mother, I didn't get to go to the movies. Being left out of the movies was still better than having to live with Her. I don't remember much about Friday evening.

On Saturday morning, after breakfast, I was with a group of girls that was taken to the YWCA to swim in their pool and to play Ping-Pong and other table games. We got to stay at the Y most of the day.

Saturday evening was dinner in the dining room of the Mark Hopkins again. The newspaper people were no longer hanging around.

Sunday morning came with breakfast, once again, in the big dining room with white table clothes and big stiff cloth napkins under the flatware. Post Toasties came to the table in a cardboard cereal bowl.

After breakfast, the station wagons were filled with people going to churches of their choice. I went with the Catholic kids and women because I was familiar with Saint Brigit Church on Van Ness Avenue. I did have to borrow a scarf to cover my head. When mass was over, we were taken back to the hotel.

When we returned from church, we were told to go to the rooms we had been staying in and gather our belongings to get ready to go home. About noon, the bus with the big Red Cross on it arrived near the main door of the hotel. We boarded the bus, were counted and had our names checked off a list and were soon on our way to Pier 4.

We sat in the bus, on the dock until we could see the boat coming around the east side of the Island. We walked to our place along the dock railing, youngest near the front of the line, and waited.

As I remember, it was very quiet in that line. Most of us knew something very big had happened, but we had no idea of how that event would affect our lives.

When the Warden Johnston docked at Pier 4, about a dozen officers, who lived in town, got off the boat. I don't remember how they looked, but I now know they must have been very tired as they had been on duty since Thursday afternoon.

The boat trip home was the longest ten minutes of our lives. The weather was lovely, warm and clear. There was not much talking. I sat outside on the back of the boat. A lot of us sat out there. It felt like we would somehow be home faster if we could see the Island in the bay.

When the boat docked, we got off according to the rules, then walked up through the metal detector, as the dock officer moved our identity cards from the "Off the Island" side of the file to the "On the Island" side.

Once through that process, I ran to the stairs and took the steps, two at a time, all the way up to the first balcony, around the far corner of the balcony and up the irregular steps to the parade ground and along the sidewalk to the porch of the little white wood sided cottage I lived in with my dad. As I stepped on the porch, I noticed several bullet holes in the white painted wood frame of the porch. I opened the door and went right into the area where the beds stood, and around the corner into the living room. The house was empty. Pop wasn't home yet. I walked over to the radio and turned it on. I have always filled the emptiness with radio music.

ALCATRAZ: My Home Town

I made myself a peanut butter and jelly sandwich and ate it. I looked in the refrigerator for milk, but the milk poured out in chunks and I didn't like what I saw.

I pulled out my drawing pad from the stack on the coffee table and doodled with a number 2 pencil. It felt so good to be home.

Pop came in about three in the afternoon. He said he was exhausted and just wanted a cup of hot coffee and a bath before going to bed. He explained that when the alarm sounded announcing the attempted break, he was ordered to the inmates' yard, on the west side of the Island, behind the prison.

Officers brought inmates from the industry buildings in groups. Any inmate working on a crew outside the prison was brought to Pop in the yard. He stayed in the yard with all the inmates who were not inside the prison. He said they all took very good care of each other.

He explained that when it got cold at night, the inmates formed a circle around him and took turns moving from the outside of the circle to the inside of the circle.

Pop called the inmates "my boys." He knew each of them by name. He also knew their record leading up to Alcatraz and yet, could find something positive about each of them.

It was after he told me about his time during the riot that he told me about Mr. Stites and Mr. Miller. He said he was not worried about the Millers as he knew they had family back East who would help them find a place to live.

He did say he was concerned about Betsy Stites as she and her children had no family on the West coast. As one of the officers in the Officer's Club, he was thinking about what could be done to help Betsy and the children.

After his bath, he went to bed and I could hear him snore as I listened to the Sunday evening mystery theater, Fibber McGee and Molly, Jack Benny and the other Sunday radio shows.

The Federal Government rules did not allow the families of employees to live on Alcatraz after the death of that employee. Each grieving family was allowed three days to make other living arrangements. They had to pack and be off the Federal Reservation at the end of the third day.

At the next Officers Club meeting, the club received a bill from the American Red Cross. It was an itemized statement of the expense of caring for the women and children, from Thursday evening until Sunday afternoon and included the rooms and meals at the Mark Hopkins Hotel, the most expensive hotel in San Francisco at that time. It was then that the officers voted to set aside the bill from the Red Cross and use that money, instead, to help the Stites family and the Miller family. The American Red Cross was notified that they would not be paid and that if they persisted, a letter would be written to the editors of each San Francisco newspaper.

ALCATRAZ: My Home Town

The Officers Club took up a collection, which added up to $6,900. That money was divided in half and $3,450 was given to each family.

Several of the officers helped Betsy Stites buy property in Santa Rosa, California. The officers then built the Stites family a three-bedroom home on the large acreage where Betsy was able to raise pigs and goats. She also had a milking cow and a crop of alfalfa, which she could harvest to feed the animals. She had a large number of egg laying chickens and was able to sell eggs in the community.

The Stites family did fine. For two summers, the Alcatraz kids would spend time camping out on the Stites farm as some of the officers improved the buildings on the place.

The Stites farm gave the Alcatraz kids a chance to learn about where chickens, milk and eggs come from. The Stites remained a part of the Alcatraz family.

WHAT THE DADS DID

We were kids. We had no idea what kind of work our dads did. When I saw my dad working as the boat officer, I could watch him work and then I knew what he was doing. When he left home at 7 AM and was gone all day long, out of sight, I had no idea that he might be in harms way.

During the Alcatraz riot of 1946, my dad was working in the carpentry shop with nine inmates. I did not know how close to violence he might have been. Were those inmates behaving well to minimize their time in the Federal Prison system? Would any of them attack him or use him as a hostage? It was many years later that I began to think about how my father and the fathers of my friends made a living.

Alcatraz Island Prison came about directly because of the Mob, which developed during the Prohibition period in America. Several times, when the Mob leaders were placed in prison, they paid money to the officers and lived like kings during the prison time. The Mob members would visit as ordered by the bosses, and the time in prison might just as well have been spent in a fine hotel room.

ALCATRAZ: My Home Town

The Federal Bureau of Prisons decided that the military prison at Alcatraz Island would be perfect for their needs. Around 1933, as the military prisoners were moved to other prisons, the Federal Bureau of Prisons took over Alcatraz.

To be held at Alcatraz Island, a federal prisoner had to have made several attempts to escape from other federal prisons, or the government had good reason to believe their gang might try to break him out of prison.

The officers who worked in the Federal Bureau of Prisons had to pass college equivalency tests to qualify for the job. Physical fitness and shooting knowledge were essential. Ranks were very much like the military ranks. Training officers moved up to "Junior Officer" then with the passage of time and an increase of skills, "Senior Officer." Again, experience and more tests, one could move up to Lieutenant, then Captain, to Associate Warden and then, the highest rank, Warden.

My dad looked great in his prison uniform. The charcoal black dress suit fit him well. The light grey colored dress shirt with the dark dress tie, tied with a large knot, was just his style. When he relaxed, the tie was loosened just a bit and the top button of the shirt was undone. He would unbutton the cuffs and fold them up one turn.

Alcatraz held about two hundred and fifty inmates at the highest population. These men were among the most dangerous because their goal was, mostly, to escape.

ALCATRAZ: My Home Town

Harold L. Henry, Sr. in his
federal prison officer's uniform

During this time in our history, there was a general belief that criminals could be rehabilitated. Because of this belief in rehabilitation, the prisoners at Alcatraz were taught some skills in industry. The industries included laundry, where not only the laundry for Alcatraz officers and families was done, but laundry was also done for the two major bases in the area, the Presidio and the base on Angel Island. In the wood shop, desks, hat racks and desk chairs were made for military bases and other federal office buildings. The dry cleaners and the tailor shop were close together. There was a door mat shop and a rope shop. The dock crew inmates were supervised in painting, electrical repair, garbage collection, milk delivery and other skills related to home care for the residents of the island.

The officers who instructed the inmates in the industrial skills were specialists in those skills and worked Monday through Friday.

Correctional officers, like my dad, were to supervise the inmates at all times and keep close tabs on the men they were supervising. None of the officers in contact with inmates wore guns. Guns were kept up in the towers or the gun galleries where the inmates could not get to them.

Most of our dads worked three or four months on the day shift, then a rotation to the evening shift, then three or four months later, a rotation to the night shift. Officers who preferred the night shift were more than welcomed to stay on the night shift.

When my dad worked the day shift, he was home at dinnertime and we would fix dinner and eat together. I would wash the dishes and he would dry them. After dinner he would also read from the newspaper for me or read a book to me over a period of time.

When he worked the evening shift, I saw him only on his days off. I had to fix my own dinner, often a peanut butter and jelly sandwich and a big glass of milk. I could buy milk at the canteen any time I needed to.

Milk, on Alcatraz, was easier to get than when I lived on the farm. No cow to milk, no cream to separate for sale and no need to worry about ice for the icebox. As I got older, I would fix canned soup for dinner and enjoy it with crackers.

When Pop worked the night shift, I was asleep when he left for work and he would arrive home just before I left for school. He slept during the day, when all the kids were in school. The evening was ours to share. I liked having him around during my evenings at home.

Pop was a sociable guy. He enjoyed playing poker with a small group of other correctional officers who lived on the island with their families. The card players included the Peppers, the Martins and Irving Levenson, among others. The games were penny ante, so even when he lost, it was not a great amount.

Some of the other officers and their wives had a bridge group, which met regularly. At least once a month he would spend his days off in town with one of his lady friends. He had several lady friends over the years when he was a single parent. If I asked about where he was and what he did, he would tell me. If I didn't ask, he didn't offer the information.

When he went to town, he was always dressed in a suit and tie. His shoes would be polished and he kept that top button of his shirt buttoned while in public.

One of my favorite officers was Lt. Rychner. He used to tell me that because I was pigeon toed, I would grow up to play golf like Babe Didrikson Zaharias. Rychner went to town to play golf at least one day a week for as long as I can remember. Although he loved children, he and his wife, Bee, had none.

Another of my officer friends was Floyd Fisher. He had a lot to do with me choosing to go into nurses' training. He helped me decide on my future, and then helped me find a school in our area, that had dormitory living, so I could go away to college. Most of his spare time was spent reading.

Jim Hudson was another officer who became a friend. He maintained contact with me through his moves to Terminal Island and into his retirement years in Redding California. He encouraged my intellectual drive.

There were strict rules about no personal involvement with an inmate. A few officers breached that rule, were caught and dismissed from the prison service. I remember a story about one of the officers who mailed a letter for an inmate, outside the prison. Eventually he was caught and was terminated. The inmate told on the officer who had done him a "favor".

Several of the younger officers looked up to my Pop and would come to our place to talk to him. When they did, he would put on a pot of coffee and sit at the kitchen table to talk.

At the kitchen table, the top button of his shirt was undone, his tie was loosened and his shirt cuffs were turned up one turn.

ANOTHER MOVE

It was a weekend in June. Soon, school would be out for the summer. The Alcatraz kids had spent the morning roller-skating on the big parade ground, near the hardball court building. I was getting better at roller-skating but had broken another pair of skates on this day.

The other kids had gone home to have lunch. I walked to the little parade ground, then down the long, uneven concrete steps, along the fence to the first balcony where the canteen was. Between the stairway and the #64 building's stonewall, the storekeeper had tossed wooden crates. Many of the supplies had been shipped to the Island in these same crates.

The assortment of wood was a wonder. In a very short time I was able to collect parts of boxes and drop the parts into a bigger box. I pulled the bigger box full of parts up the stairs onto the little parade ground and across to the sidewalk leading to the little white cottage.

I left the box on the sidewalk when I went into the cottage to pull our hammer from the tool drawer, in the little kitchen. Now I could put my idea into motion.

Using the long 1" by 3" as the center of the vehicle, I banged out a seat using the orange crate end and placed that seat on one end of the board. Then I nailed another long 1" by 3", centered to the back end of the first board. The roller skate came apart in the middle. To nail the two wheels of each skate to the board, I had to flatten the upper portion of the skate. It was much easier to flatten the front of each skate than it was to flatten the back of the skate.

The nails would not go through the metal of the skate, so I attached the wheels by hammering the nails around the metal and bending them overthe metal of the skate. The backs of the skates were on the backboard and the front of the skates were on the front board. The "go-cart" was coming together. The big problem was that I had no drill, nor did I have a bolt to use as a center for the front to allow the "go-cart" to turn. Oh well, we'll just have to ride in a straight line.

I used an old jump rope for the "steering handle" by attaching each end of the rope to opposite sides of the front axle and holding the middle with both hands while scooting myself along the big parade ground.

It was about this time that a new girl came over to me. She and her family had just moved into the apartment where Herbie Stites had lived with his family. Her name was Janet Moore.

She offered to push me on the cart. That was fun for one short trip, then it was my turn to push her. The cart made it for about ten feet, then Janet tried to use the rope to guide the cart and the force pulled the front axle off the body of the "go cart". The go-cart didn't go anymore.

ALCATRAZ: My Home Town

The uneven steps to the canteen.

Janet and I picked up the pieces and put them in a garbage can near the steps to her apartment. She explained that her family had come from another Federal Prison and her family had waited until school was out to move to the Island. She went on to explain that she had a younger sister, Myrna, who was my age.

Over the coming years, we would all become very close friends. Pop came home early in the month of June and said that a different apartment had come available in #64 building and that we were going to move to that apartment. He explained that I would be able to have a room of my own and that it would be quieter, so when he had to sleep during the day, it would be easier.

The move was very easy. We had no furniture to move. We moved the kitchenware and our clothing.

The new place was on the second floor of old #64 building, on the backside. Our apartment windows looked out at the concrete walls under the little parade ground. By hanging out of the living room window, I could look down one story to see the iron bars of the grill we called "China Town".

The door to this apartment was inserted into a short hallway. The door opened into the kitchen area. It was a very large area with a nook for the dining table and chairs around the corner to the left.

The electric stove was on the west wall of the kitchen area. Pop kept his black cast iron frying pan on the stove. Every piece of meat he cooked was cooked, in that frying pan. The cupboards were on the north wall. There were two big windows in the kitchen area.

The living room was one third of the apartment. As with most of the floors in this building, the hard wood had been painted with gray paint. Our rug, which had moved from outside the fence, then to the cottage, now sat in the apartment in #64 building. Pops' big easy chair was near the living room entry door wall, with his footstool near the chair. There was a tall shaded lamp light on the right side of his chair. His habit of reading the newspaper every evening continued for as long as I can remember.

On the far wall of the living room was a couch to match the color of the easy chair. Near the couch were my brother, Harold's, phonograph and his record collection. Near there was a highly polished, dark wood table with the old radio on it.

There were three radiators in that apartment. Each radiator was under a window.

In the bedroom, which became mine, there was a framed, white wood closet, which, with great effort, could be moved about the room. The bed frame was of the same dark colored wood as the other furniture. It was a double bed. There were two big pillows on the government issued mattress.

The bathroom had one door that opened into my new bedroom and another door that opened into the wide hallway where Pop would set his single bed.

That hallway did have a closet built into the wall, so Pop could hang his uniforms and suits. At the head of his bed, he used a footstool for his alarm clock and ashtray. He was able to hang a reading lamp from the wall to the right, so he could read in bed. There was a doorway opening into the hall near the head of his bed. That door was left open all the time.

The tall dark wooden chest of drawers he placed about two feet from the foot of his bed.

On our next trip to town, her bought a pair of red curtains from Woolworth's. One of the pair he hung behind his chest of drawers, across the hallway to make his area look homier. The other curtain was hung over the kitchen entry to the hallway near the apartment main door.

At the same time, he bought the curtains, he allowed me to buy a gallon of pink paint and a gallon of light blue paint so I could paint my room. I measured and drew a line half way up the wall of the room. The bottom half I painted blue. The top half was pink. Paint rollers were not in use yet, so the whole job was done by hand brushing.

I arranged my room with the bed at the end near the bathroom door. The white closet was moved to the wall on the right of the window, so sunlight could come into my room. I had a fancy, mahogany dresser with a big mirror and raised drawers on each side. The middle drawer of the dresser became my desk drawer with pencils, rulers and art equipment. The drawers on each side became the place for underwear and clothing that could not be hung in the closet.

I loved having my new room all to myself. I made the bed and put pillowcases on the pillows. Then when it was time for me to go to sleep at night, I would pull a second blanket up over my body for the night. That way, I didn't have to make my bed every day.

I usually fell asleep at night listening to the radio.

It was summer and the officers going up to the Stites farm, in Santa Rosa, had invited me to join with some of the other Alcatraz children for a week on the farm. Pop said I could go and told me we would have to go to town to buy a sleeping bag, as the kids were sleeping in two tents on the property.

He reminded me to be sure to pack jeans, shirts and several changes of underwear. I could hardly wait.

STAY AT THE STITES' FARM

School was finally out for the summer. The last school day was in the middle of the week. Pop was off the next day, so we went to town to buy a few things for my trip to the Stites' farm in Santa Rosa.

It had been explained to us that there were two camping tents set up, one for boys and the other for girls. The Alcatraz officers, who were working to build the farmhouse and out buildings, would be staying in the larger tent. The tent for the girls was a four-person, three windows, and green canvas unit. The big tent held about ten cots with bedrolls or sleeping bags on them. The boys who slept in the men's tent, slept on the ground in their sleeping bags.

On this day, Pop and I took the streetcar to Market Street, near the Civic Center. When we got off, we headed southwest, toward Octavia. Pop said, "We're looking for an Army surplus store." We only had to walk about five blocks before we found what Pop was looking for.

Inside the store, Pop asked the clerk to show us some of the sleeping bags. The biggest bag was a long flat rectangle in light brown material. It had layers of material, like a big ugly quilt, which opened by way of a very long zipper from the bottom and up the side, to the top.

The second bag was shaped like a big person, narrow at the bottom, getting wider toward the top, then a cone shape where the head was supposed to fit, with a cutout for the face.

The second bag looked like it would be the easiest to take care of and to sleep in, so that's the one Pop got for me.

When we finished shopping, we dropped in to the Mayflower Restaurant for a snack before going back to the dock to catch a boat home.

Packing was easy. I grabbed a pillowcase from the linen closet, in the bathroom, and put my stuff in it. The stuff included a pair of coveralls, a pair of jeans, several pairs of panties, some blouses and a couple of pairs of sox. With my new "mummy" bag, I would have only two bundles to take with me on the trip to Santa Rosa.

Mr. Bergen was the driver. His daughter, Kay, rode with Betty Lou Orr and me in the back seat. Mr. Orr was the other man going on the trip. His son, Bobby Joe, rode in the front seat with the men.

Everything looked familiar as the car moved along Van Ness Avenue to Lombard Street, where we turned right and headed for the Golden Gate Bridge. Mr. Bergen stopped at the tollgate to give money to the attendant. From the bridge, we could see Alcatraz in the middle of San Francisco Bay.

The drive wandered through Marin County, along Richardson's Bay, on past Corte Madera, Cotati, Rohnert Park and finally, to Santa Rosa. Just inside the city limits, we turned off the main highway and found our way to Stony Point Road. Mr. Bergen had been there before, so he knew his way very well.

Kay Bergan, one of the kids riding in the back seat on the way to the Stites' property

ALCATRAZ: My Home Town

When we arrived at the property, Mr. Bergen pulled his car right up onto the front area, just in front of the biggest tent. We all got out of the car and stretched our legs. The trunk of the car was unpacked. Each of us got some bundles with directions of where to take each.

Betty, Kay and I each placed our bundles in the girls' tent. Then we ran to the house to find the bathroom. The house was unfinished, inside and out. The bathroom had the necessary toilet, washbasin and tub; however, the walls were unpainted sheetrock and the wood door was nude. The roll of tissue sat on the back of the toilet.

Betsy Stites welcomed us with glasses of lemonade and showed us to a table on the unfinished screened in front porch where we could sit and drink the treat as she talked with us.

She took us on a tour of the home being built by the officers. The kitchen was big and modern with a gas range and a large refrigerator placed conveniently near cupboards, and a large sink and drain board. The kitchen was the only finished room in the house. The walls were painted a glossy white, as were the cupboards.

Her bedroom was near the kitchen, and was furnished with a double bed, a dresser and a chest of drawers.

Down the hall was a room for Herbie and his two brothers. There was a bunk bed in that room and a single bed near the window. There were two chests of drawers.

The third bedroom was for Thelma, Herbie's sister. It was the smallest bedroom. The furniture consisted of a single bed, a dresser and a chest of drawers.

In a short time, the men and boys joined us. It was about this time that Herbie showed up. He had been at a neighboring farm when he saw the car drive up.

Mr. Bergen made sure we understood the limits. He made some rules that we were expected to live by while we were on the farm. The rules included meal times, cleaning up after wards, bed times and general behavior.

Herbie led us outside to take us on a tour of the farm. We walked over to the pigpen. It was just beyond the back kitchen door. The pig trough had been cleaned of the pig slop that had been delivered from the house that morning.

Two of the sows were very fat. Herbie explained that baby pigs would be born "...any day now."

Past the pigs, toward the east was a cow stall in front of a high feeding trough. To protect the cow, more from the direct sunlight, than anything else, there was a slanted roof of about ten feet by ten feet, up on four thick posts. There was thin wire fencing around the cow pasture.

North of the pig pen and on the west side of the cow pen, was a good sized hen house with several

ALCATRAZ: My Home Town

layers of nesting places for the chickens to lay their eggs. The place was laid out so Betsy could collect eggs twice daily. There were a couple of roosters walking around in the yard clucking proudly.

Between the front edge of the cow pen up to Stony Point Road, the earth had been planted in alfalfa. The farming equipment had been parked to the east of the cow pen.

Someone explained that the barn was the project of this week. More help would be coming up from the Alcatraz, over the next few days. Mr. Orr and Mr. Bergen were going to nail together the frames for the four walls, so the barn could be raised when help arrived.

In what seemed like no time, we were asked to help with the dinner. Kay and I set the table for everyone. Just ten places this evening. The flatware was only a knife and a fork. We had no need for spoons.

The dinner was wonderful! It was served family style, by passing bowls of food from person to person with each taking a portion. The meat was fried chicken. Before we took a bite, Mr. Bergen led us in prayer.

After dinner, we helped wash and dry the dishes while the boys went out to feed the animals. Herbie's big brother milked the cow and brought the milk into the kitchen for Mrs. Stites to separate the cream.

Not long after dinner, it began to get dark. We were tired and decided to go to bed early. We went to our tent to dress for bed and climbed into our sleeping bags. It was too warm in my bag, so I left the top unsnapped and slept with my head outside the hooded portion of the bag. I used the case with my clothes in it for a pillow. Sleep came quickly.

After breakfast, the next morning, we went exploring along the road. On the property next door, near Stony Point Road, there was an old tumbled down pump house next to a large metal water tank. The pump house was two stories tall, and there was a ladder inside, leading up to the top floor.

The boys had beaten us there and were throwing eggs against the old battered walls of the pump house. They had taken them from a nest in the old building. When the eggs hit the wall, instead of bright yellow and snotty stuff, there were fist sized black shiny lumps. Closer examination revealed dead baby birds. I wanted to cry. Oh! Those poor little babies.

The boys ran off to do something else. That's when I went into the old place and climbed the ladder to the second floor. There, on a board near the window was a pigeon nest. It had an egg in it. I took the egg in my hand and carefully climbed down the ladder.

I went back to the girls' tent and gently placed the egg in the corner of my sleeping bag. I wanted to keep it warm, like a mother bird would keep her eggs warm. I didn't tell anyone what I had done.

We were busy the rest of the day. Sometimes helping with the farm work, sometimes playing and following the directions of any adult who asked us to do something.

When it was time for bed that night, I got into my sleeping bag and put the egg in my right armpit. I slept very soundly. The following morning, when I woke, there was a little soft ball of yellow feathers in that place in my sleeping bag. I lifted the little creature with one hand and held him close to my body. The empty cracked eggshell could be cleaned up later. I had a hungry baby bird.

When I got to the house, I asked Mrs. Stites if I could have a piece of bread and some milk in a glass. She got the milk and bread for me. I offered the bird the bread, then the milk. He did not seem to know how to eat. That's when I mixed the bread and milk in the glass, then held the semi liquid in my right hand. I pushed the baby bird's head into my food filled cupped hand. He ate until he could hold no more. Then he fell asleep in my hand.

Mrs. Stites found an old oatmeal box that I carved into nest for the baby bird. I found some clean straw in the chicken house to put in the bottom of the box and put the baby bird there to rest between meals.

About four times a day, for the rest of the week, I fed the baby bird on milk and bread. The cute little critter was growing and the other kids began to care about it. We named the bird Windy.

It was a wonder filled week at the Stites farm. When the week was over, Mr. Bergen helped me find a shoebox so I could take Windy home to Alcatraz with us. This was the beginning of another wonderful adventure on Alcatraz.

WINDY, MY PET PIGEON

I had brought Windy home with me from the week stay at the Stites' farm. He was beginning to change from the soft yellow fuzzy feathers of a helpless baby bird to the darker grey and black feathers of the older bird. He was very tame, having been around people from his first day out of the egg. He lived under my bed in the back of our second-floor apartment in old #64 building.

At least four times a day I would make squishy bread and milk, which I would hold in my cupped hand and Windy would push his head into the circular opening made by my thumb and index finger. He would fill his beak with the stuff, then pull his head out and point his beak toward the ceiling so he could swallow the stuff. As he did this, the craw, at the front of his chest would grow fat.

Most of the time, I would feed him while sitting at the table in our kitchen. When Pop was home for dinner, Windy would eat with us at the dinner table. After dinner, Windy would hop down from the table and walk around our living quarters. When he got tired, he would return to his living quarters under my bed.

Midway through summer vacation, a new family moved into the apartment on the second floor on the west side of our old building. The Shield family had two girls, Joanne and Patty. Joanne was just a bit younger than I. She was a girlie girl and wore dresses every day.

The first time I met the new girls, I was up on the little parade ground. They had dolls and buggies and were pretending to be mothers to the dolls.

A short time after meeting them, Joanne suggested we play jacks. I remembered the game from the third grade in Douglas. I had never played jacks before. Joanne taught me how to play. We played for several hours, then their mother called the girls in for lunch and an afternoon rest.

Now and then, Joanne would come to our apartment to play or to look at our "Life' magazine. She noticed that I didn't have any dolls and asked why. I don't remember what I told her. I am sure I made it clear that I didn't want any dolls!

One day, Joanne was visiting when we heard her mother up on the little parade ground, calling her kids to come home for lunch. Joanne left and as she climbed the stairs up to the parade ground, her mother asked her where she had been. She told her mom that she had been inside our apartment. Her mother said, "I don't want you to go there again. There is no mother in that home." I remember feeling hurt and very puzzled about what having a "mother in that home" had to do with anything.

Near the end of summer, Pop took me to the Mission district for school shopping. Edna and her daughter, Dorothy helped me buy the usual underwear, socks, shoes, skirts and sweaters. Shopping was never one of my favorite things to do. It was nice to have a grown up help me select clothing and make sure it would fit for the year ahead. All the socks were the same color so if one got lost in the prison laundry, there would still be another sock to make a pair.

It would be another year at Sherman school for most of the Alcatraz kids not in Catholic schools. On the first day of school, Mrs. Shields accompanied Joanne and Patty up the hill to catch a streetcar. We saw her, later, in the hall of Sherman school.

When school was out, they joined the rest of the Alcatraz kids on the walk down to Pier 4.

Sunday school was back in session as there were now enough kids to make it worthwhile.

Once every two weeks, the residents of Alcatraz got to watch a free big screen movie. I think the first movie I saw there was "Going My Way" with Bing Crosby, Barry Fitzgerald and some child actors. The prison inmates got to see the movie on Saturday afternoon. The residents got to go up to the prison auditorium on Sunday evenings to see it.

ALCATRAZ: My Home Town

Soon after Halloween, that year, I decided to change my room around. What a surprise when I moved my bed! There on the floor was a collection of pigeon poop as long and as wide as the shadow of my double bed on the floor. It had been collecting since the day I brought Windy home with me.

I don't remember any smell. I do remember that it took hours and a lot of scrubbing to get the pigeon poop off the floor! Time to make some changes, I decided. Windy needed a place to poop that wasn't under my bed.

I went to the stairway, just off the little parade ground, that lead down to the back of the Canteen. There I found a couple of wooden crates in good condition. I took the two crates back to our place and found our hammer. The construction project resulted in a new home for Windy. With great effort, I raised the window, in our living room, about two feet. While holding the window up with one hand, I set the wooden crate in the area between the bottom of the window and the seal. The position of the box would allow Windy to sleep in the warm, lined side of the crate or to be in the opened non-lined area over hanging the outside of the building.

Windy had moved from a diet of milk and bread, to walnuts, then to canary food. The canary food was purchased at the dime store, in the Marina district in San Francisco. To make sure he had food and water, I wired two empty tin cans to the crate. The old green bean can was for water. The little stubby old tuna can was for birdseed. Windy seemed to get used to the new living area. He was beginning to fly around the area outside.

One day, Joanne's mother complained to my father that the pigeon had landed on her windowsill and pecked on the pie she had set in the window to cool.

Christmas came. Pop and I got our Christmas tree. He and I decorated it with the ornaments he stored somewhere. I made the angel, for the top of the tree, out of the cardboard toilet paper center and white toilet paper. There were not many presents under the tree. Pop counted on the Santa Claus who lived in the lighthouse to fill my stocking with candy and fruit and nuts.

Pop had to be at work at seven in the morning on Christmas Day, so he was not home when I woke. There was a gift for me, sitting on one of the tree branches. I just had to open it! I knew I should wait for Pop, but I just couldn't.

I unwrapped it very carefully. Inside the gift-wrap was a brown colored leather box with a flip top. I opened that top and found a lady's wristwatch. I was more than disappointed! I don't know what I wanted, but a wristwatch was nowhere on my list.

So he wouldn't know what I had done, I rewrapped the gift. When Pop got home, I pretended to be excited when I unwrapped it the second time. Pop loved his new tie. At least he acted like he was really surprised!

ALCATRAZ: My Home Town

Soon after Christmas, the Shield family moved to the other side of the Island, into "C" building. We'd still see each other and play together. When they moved from the next-door apartment, an inmate crew repainted the place.

The New Year arrived. 1947 brought many new adventures.

Windy was growing a raised area of light blue color over the top of his beak, near his head and his feathers were beginning to shine with the colors of the rainbow. His flying had improved and he could be seen begging for food on the parade ground now and then.

The Fisher family moved into the apartment next door. They had two older boys, one away at college, and the other in the Army. Mom Fisher invited me in to learn how to make snicker doodles, a special cinnamon flavored cookie, her boys liked. She would be sending them cookies now and then.

Mom Fisher, without knowing it, taught me a lot about how good wives treat their husbands. She would make sure all the housework was done before her husband was home from the job. She put the newspaper near his reading chair. While he relaxed after a day at work, she prepared dinner and set the table.

"C" Building is where the Orrs, the Moudes, and the Hacks lived. Sunday school was held on the top floor (left side)

She taught me about what a "balanced meal" means. She also made sure I knew the importance of "thank you" notes and other general courtesies.

The winter passed quickly and spring arrived.

It was near Easter vacation. Windy was gone for twenty-four hours. I was really worried about him.

Pop and I talked over dinner on that evening. Pop advised me that birds like to mate in the spring of the years and that Windy was old enough to mate. Before that time, I had never given any thought to Windy mating.

When Windy came home, I was so happy to see him. I gave him extra walnuts that evening.

ALCATRAZ: My Home Town

The next day, when I got home, Windy was not there. He was gone again and this time, he didn't come home, ever.

Now, wherever I visit the Palace of Fine Arts, in the Marina District, near Lombard Street, when I see a male pigeon with gray and black feathers, I pretend it is one of the descendants of Windy, my pet pigeon.

THE BICYCLE

During my time in Berkeley, at Uncle Donald's house, my cousin Charley would let me ride his bike around on McGee Street, in front of the old two story white house. He had a boy's bike, so the bar was across the top from the handle bar holder to the seat.

That area was flat. When I wanted to stop the bike, I'd throw my leg over the bar, jump off the bike, hanging onto the handlebars, and run a few steps to slow down.

During summer vacation, in 1946, Pop decided we would go bike riding in Golden Gate Park. We had to take the streetcar down Van Ness Avenue to Fulton Avenue. At Fulton, we transferred to a bus and got off near Nineteenth Avenue. On the north side of Fulton Avenue were several bike rental shops.

Pop got two bikes, one for him and a girl's bike for me. He told the shop owner when to expect us back, and we walked the bikes across the street to the entrance of the park.

Pop got on his bike and told me to follow him. After riding for half and hour, we passed the backside of the aquarium before heading for the Japanese Tea Garden. We stopped at the entrance of the tea garden and parked our bicycles. We had tea and cookies on a fancy oriental looking porch-like platform. There were Japanese lanterns moving gently with the breeze. All in all, it was a memorable experience.

When the last cookie was consumed, we headed back over the bridge and out to the sidewalk where we had left our bikes. Pop instructed me to follow him. We pumped hard for a while, then at the top of a little hill, it was no longer necessary to pump.

I passed Pop, who yelled, "Slow down!" As much as I wanted to, I had no idea how. The bike went faster and faster. I dodged a pedestrian and continued down hill and around a curve. That's when I realized I was in big trouble! Ahead of me I could see the four lane divided highway that was Nineteenth Avenue. There were no traffic lights at that time. The bicycle traveled down the hill and bounced off the curb and onto the highway pavement and quickly across all four lanes and into the curb on the far side of the street. The bike hit the curb hard and threw me over the handlebars onto the sidewalk. I skinned knees, elbows and forehead. I would not cry!

Pop stopped his bike at the corner, dismounted and waited for the cars to pass. He walked to where I was sprawled on the ground and asked if he could help me up. It was several minutes before I could answer. Things just hurt too much. Finally, I got up.

He hugged me and said, "Don't you know where the brakes are?"

"Brakes?" I responded. "I didn't know bikes have brakes."

He told me to watch him. He mounted his bike and rode a short distance, then said, "When I push the pedals backward, the brakes are applied and I can slow down or I can stop."

Then he told me to try the same thing. It worked! My bike had brakes.

We got back to the bike rental shop and Pop paid the nice man for the time we had used the bikes. He asked the man to check out the bike I had ridden and told him of the accident. The man said the bike was fine. He and Pop shook hands and we headed back to the bus stop on the south side of Fulton Avenue to catch the bus toward Van Ness Avenue.

All the connections were just right and we caught the afternoon boat back to Alcatraz.

As soon as we were in our apartment, Pop made me wash the scrapes and scratches. When he thought the skin was clean enough, he applied a dose of iodine to "prevent infection." The maroon colored medicine stung something awful.

It was a day I will never forget. About the middle of August, Pop took me to town again. He had decided that I needed a bicycle. We went to a shop in the Marina District and looked at their inventory. The most affordable bike was a "Phillips" from England. The shop owner asked me to take it out on the sidewalk and try riding it. He explained that the brakes were the handgrips on the handlebars. He went on to show me which handgrip worked which brake. The sidewalk was almost empty. The bike was easy to ride. Pop paid the man cash for the bicycle and we left the shop with my new English racing bike.

Now we had an interesting challenge. The big parade ground on Alcatraz is about a mile and a half wide. There is not a lot of room for bicycle riding. Pop had another idea. He said, "Follow me."

We went to Fillmore Street, then up to Bay Street where we turned right. Pop walked while I rode my new English racing bike up to a corner, turned around, then back. On the north side of Bay Street, we turned left on Webster Street. As soon as we turned there I knew we were headed to Grandpa Henry's place. He had a garage.

Pop opened the gate to the outdoor stairway. At the top of the stairs he rang the doorbell. Marie, Grandpa's second wife, answered the door. As soon as she saw Pop, she invited him in. Pop said he had something to show the Colonel, my grandpa.

In the afternoon, Grandpa usually sat in his study reading the latest medical journals or other medical information. Marie called the Colonel to the front door.

Bill's wife Clair, Bill Henry, my father,
and me on my Aunt Eleanor's bike

He came down the stairs with Pop behind him. Right away he noticed me on the bicycle. I sat the bike against the wall so I could hug Grandpa. He liked being hugged.

Pop explained the situation about the need for a place to keep the bike. Grandpa explained, to me, that I could certainly keep my bicycle in his garage. He stressed the need to close the little garage door firmly when I got my bike out, and again when I put my bike back into the garage after using it. He added there would be no need to make much noise, or to ring the bell.

I put my new English racing bike in Grandpa's garage, shut the door firmly and joined Grandpa and Marie for hot tea in Grandpa's study.

When the visit was over, Pop and I walked to the dock for the afternoon boat back home to Alcatraz.

Betty Orr (far left) and Agie Mouder (far right)

My first boyfriend, Ed Faulk, walked to
Windfield Scott School with me

ALCATRAZ: My Home Town

It must have been after Easter vacation in 1947, when I asked Pop if I could bring my bike home to Alcatraz. The conversation was rather short. "It's your bike. You take care of it and you can bring it home."

The next day I went to Grandpa's, got my bike and rode it to Pier 4. It was so nice to know how to work the brakes on this bike. Because of the steepness of the hill, down to the dock, I had to zigzag down the long hill.

The boat officer helped me get the bicycle down the gangplank and onto the Warden Johnston. Of course, he also had to help get it off the boat once we reached the Island.

The dock officer encouraged me to take the bike on the bus, up the road to the gate, where he unlocked the gate so I could push it onto the little parade ground.

It was early afternoon when I arrived on the big parade ground with my bike. Within minutes, several of my teenaged friends gathered around to see and to ride the English racing bike.

It was not long before my friends all had bikes. The most popular bike was a Schwinn. Donny Hurley had a blue and white boy's Schwinn bicycle with a head light for riding after dark.

Betty Lou Orr got a bicycle for her birthday. It was also a Schwinn. Then Bobby Joe Orr got his bike, then Donny Martin and so on until most of my

Alcatraz friends had a bike. None of them had an English racing bike.

We developed games and races and competitions of all kinds to ride our bikes. The new apartment buildings had bicycles on patios and in entry hallways.

I often left my bike on the little parade ground. Taking the bike up and down the stairs was difficult and sometimes dangerous. Near the end of summer before junior high school, I lost interest in riding my English racing bike. By the time my brother, Harold, returned from WWII, my bike was stashed in my bedroom. It stood in the corner with collected memories and dust.

When we moved to a larger apartment, in #64 Building, I took the bike back to Grandpa's garage. It must have been there the year he died, while I was away at college. I don't remember ever seeing it again.

CHANGING

Fifth grade at Sherman School was getting to be a bore. I still had difficulty reading but made good grades by joining committees for work, then volunteering to do the artwork while others worked on research and wrote the papers.

That worked very well until the spring of the year when schools administered the Iowa Test. The test, reportedly, was to evaluate individual knowledge levels. The math section was easy, and then came the part of the test where each student had to read the directions, and then follow them.

I knew I was in trouble. It was a timed test and I was not going to make time! That's when I suddenly developed "eye problems." I began to hold the test paper up in front of me, at arm's length, to read the directions. Then I would set it down on the desk and follow the directions.

About the third time I held it at arm's length, Mrs. Peara came back to my desk. She asked if I was having trouble seeing. "Oh yes" I said.

ALCATRAZ: My Home Town

At that time, she excused me from taking the rest of the test. She sent me to the library with instructions to see her at the end of the day. When I went back to her class at the end of the day, she had a note for my father.

He was surprised to get a note that said I needed an eye examination. He, of course, had not noticed any problem.

On his next day off, he took me to an eye doctor in the Mission District. He left me there and instructed me to meet him at Edna's when the examination was over.

I was not sure what I had to do to get eyeglasses, but I knew this was my only way out. I realized that my responses had to be consistent toward far sightedness. The challenge was trying to remember what my last response was to the same focal point in the optic lens.

After what seemed a very long time, the eye doctor said he had finished measuring and would have my glasses ready on Saturday. I could hardly wait.

On Saturday, I went to the Mission District eye doctor on my own. I let him fit the eyeglasses on my face. He warmed and bent the plastic that would go over my ears. He had me read letters of various sizes. He assured me that because of the development of plastics, the glasses were unbreakable. Then he handed me an ugly brown leather case with an eyeglass cleaning cloth folded inside. He reminded me that I only needed to use the glasses when I read. That was good news!

From that day on, while walking down the Van Ness Avenue hill, toward the dock, I would drop the glasses on the sidewalk and kick them down the hill in front of me. Now and then I would step on them. I was hoping they would break. They never did. They really were "unbreakable!" I ended up having to wear them every "reading time" at Sherman School.

During the summer, I talked to Pop about letting me change schools for the sixth grade. I really wanted to go to Winfield Scott School. Eddie Faulk went there and he really liked it, I confided to Pop. He responded, "It's your education. If you think Winfield Scott is a better school, go there in September."

The first thing I did after that conversation was to find my eyeglass case and stash it in a bottom drawer, never to have to open it again.

Winfield Scott School is close to the Palace of Fine Arts, in San Francisco's Marina District.

Most mornings, Eddie Faulk and I would walk up the Van Ness Avenue hill very quickly, then turn right on Bay Street. We kept up the fast pace past the bay side of the junior high school, where Bay Street turns slightly toward the Golden Gate Bridge and led us to North Point. At North Point, we turned left a block or two to the school. Because we left Alcatraz on the 7:20 launch, we were often the first kids in the fenced, blacktopped yard. Once there, we usually pretended not to know each other. After all, sixth grade is too early for boyfriend/ girlfriend relationships.

The kids in this school were different. Many were the children of career military fathers, who lived at the Presidio of San Francisco. The other children had wealthy parents. Some lived in those houses near Yacht Harbor. When you drive toward the Golden Gate Bridge at night, you can look into the big bay windows. There you could see the well lit, beautifully furnished rooms where there are no people. Many of the wealthy children I became friends with had nannies.

This allowed me a variety of experiences I would not have had, had I stayed at Sherman School.

Sixth grade and I was one of the tallest girls in the class. I knew that because we had a class picture taken and I had to stand in the back row with mostly boys.

I learned to play basketball and because of my height, and my athletic ability, I got to be very good at it. I played basketball at lunchtime and at recess.

When school was over, Eddie and I would meet at the far end of the schoolyard for the walk to the dock. One of our favorite activities, while making our way to Pier Four, was throwing dirt clods at each other. He had a great throwing arm. Oh well, the dirt brushed off with just a brief dusting.

Late in that year, before Christmas vacation, my body began to change. My chest became tender to touch and sometimes running, during basketball, it would feel like my chest was jiggling. When it jiggled, it hurt.

Aunt Eleanor had noticed my chest. She told me I should talk to my dad about getting a bra. She implied, I thought, that a bra would stop the jiggling and the discomfort. That was mythical thinking.

With great awkwardness, I talked to Pop about getting me a bra. When he figured out what I was asking for, he patted me on the head and said, "Of course I can get you a bra."

Several days later, I came home from school and found a soft lavender colored paper bag on my bed. Inside was an item wrapped in white tissue paper.

I pulled the item out of the tissue and held it up by a strap. It was a beautiful, soft, silky, white bra. However, there was a problem. In the places where my just beginning to grow breasts were to be held gently, there was enough room for two volley balls. I didn't know whether to laugh or cry. It was several days before I saw Pop to tell him about the bra.

Pop was a good guy. On the following Saturday, he got up in time for us to go together to catch the ten o'clock launch to town. He said, "We will go get you that bra."

As Pop and I talked on the boat, he told me about his experience with the saleslady. "I told her that you are about her size," he said. "She picked out what she thought would be proper."

ALCATRAZ: My Home Town

We walked up the hill from the dock and caught the "F" Streetcar to Chestnut Street. About three blocks past the junior high school, we got off on the south side of the street.

The lingerie store was on the corner. As we walked in, a little bell rang for the saleswoman. She appeared from the back room. I knew instantly what had happened and I laughed out loud.

The saleswoman was my height all right! The difference was that she had breasts as large as muskmelons. When she took the bra out of the bag, she laughed too.

While Pop went across the street to a drug store, the saleswoman measured me with a tape and fitted me properly. She placed several right sized bras, wrapped nicely with tissue paper in the lavender bag. Pop came back just in time to pay for it all.

He and I celebrated over lunch at the soda fountain that day. We were celebrating the beginning of the new development.

School at Winfield Scott was much more fun. My reading skills had increased and it was easier to make friends. I spent several overnight visits with four or five of the girls in my class. Two of the girls had nannies. Two of the other girls lived in the Presidio.

In preparing for graduation from sixth grade, I was appointed the class valedictorian and had to write a speech to present at the ceremony.

For the occasion, Pop got me a special dress. It was a very grownup dress, which, I learned later had been purchased by one of his lady friends.

My friend Marie La Rocca played a special piano piece. Then it was my turn to give the memorized speech. I think I forgot several lines, however, the ceremony went well.

When the celebration was over, I said goodbye to many of my friends and went with Pop to Aunt Eleanor's' for dinner. It was a wonderful day.

EARLY TEEN YEARS

The summer of 1948 brought new friends.

The Hart family moved into the massive four or five-bedroom apartment on the third floor, east end of the old #64 Building. Their dad was a specialist of some sort. Their mom, Marie, was a stay at home mom. They had five kids, Betty, Buddy, Billy, Bobby and Barbara. The ages were from Betty, who was just a bit older than I, down to Barbara who was about two and a half.

The other new family that year was the Moore family. They lived in the apartment in #64 Building where the Stites family had lived. They had two girls, Janet, who was two years older than me. Myrna, their second daughter, and I were the same age.

In the Federal Prison system, families were often moved around, as the needs the service required the particular skills of the officer. The system was very much like the military.

Summer gave us a chance to get to know and to play with each other.

During this summer, we borrowed tennis racquets and went on the ten o'clock boat to walk up to Funston Field to play tennis. That took care of the first couple of weeks

About the second week of vacation, there was Summer School for the teenaged kids who wanted to go. The school did offer remedial reading and math, over the summer months, for those who needed more help. However, most of the students were there to broaden life experiences in arts, crafts and music.

The San Francisco schools were apparently well financed during these post war times. I loved it! I took art and drama. Those of us who went to summer school got to know the layout of the building, so the new school year was less daunting.

School started on the first Tuesday after Labor Day. Junior high started earlier than grade school. Those of us who would attend junior high, headed down to the dock to catch the 7:20 AM boat for the mainland. Most of us walked in a group to Marina Junior High School.

The Catholic kids would continue at St. Brigid School until the end of the 8th grade.

The two groups usually split off at Bay Street, with the public-school kids turning right on Bay, while the Catholic kids continued up Van Ness Avenue to St. Brigid.

Eddie Faulk and I were still boyfriend and girlfriend, so I wore his maroon windbreaker.

That group walking to school included Joe Burdett, Janet and Myrna Moore, Bud and Betty Hart, Eddie Faulk and me.

Some of the Alcatraz kids.
Forgive the writing on the photo,
this is how it came to me.

We got to school in plenty of time to find our friends and maybe even shoot a couple of baskets or finish homework before the bell rang. Homeroom was the first fifteen-minute period of the day. That was a time for attendance to be taken and for classroom elections so we could learn the basics of democracy.

Though we didn't know it at the time, we were placed in groups depending on what the educational counselor we were assigned to had decided we would want to do when we graduated from high school. One third of the seventh grade was placed in college prep education. One third of the class was placed in business preparation, and one third was in vocational studies.

Although Myrna, Bud, Eddie and I were about the same age, we were all in different homerooms. We also had different goals in life, and this school year was the beginning of the path to different careers.

For the first time in my life, what I wore to school became important. Tight, long skirts were in style. There were lots of drawbacks to the style. When I played baseball, during lunch, every time I hit the ball, I had to pull the skirt up above my knees so I could run. For basketball, the skirt had to stay above the knees.

Although we'd see each other during the day, we hung out with our school friends at class breaks and during lunch recess. Myrna and I ended up in gym class together.

After the first day of school, we all met at the Bay Street gate and walked to the dock together. All of us had a list of items we would need to buy for our new adventure in junior high school. The list included gym clothes, a shower cap for the girls, a combination lock for our locker, a binder and paper, pens and pencils. We were expected to provide our own stuff. We were also expected to cover the schoolbooks that were loaned to us for the semester.

In seventh grade, we got to explore many possibilities. Music was offered and the choice was between "Music Appreciation," "Band" or "Choir." I choose band and played clarinet. I would practice on lunch break several times a week.

The second elective was home economics, cooking or sewing. I chose sewing but ended up having to take cooking. We didn't really learn to cook. We learned about balanced diets and table setting.

The remainder of our seven-hour school day was filled in with history, English, math, and physical education.

We could play around on the way to the dock and while waiting for the boat. We often did homework on the boat so we'd have more free time after we got home to Alcatraz.

Most of us loved being with our Alcatraz friends. After I finished my chores at home, I would change into "play" clothes and go to Betty Orr's apartment with several of our other friends. We would have toast and jam or some other snack and talk about school or missing friends or other people's parents. We learned a lot about how the other kids lived.

Betty and Bobby had to have their apartment cleaned and have dinner ready to go on the table when their mom got home on the 5:30 PM boat. Because she worked in the city, she expected them to help a lot with the housework. Their big brother, Jim, went in the service about the same time my brother Harold left for the Navy.

On days when the weather was good, we'd play outside for about an hour before going home for the evening meal. Donny Hurley was still the boss of the boys who went to Catholic school with him. The boys who attended public schools were less willing to let him boss them around.

It was about this time that many of our friends began to experiment with cigarette smoking. Of course, we didn't smoke publicly. We would get together in one of the homes of a family with a working mother. Few of us had cigarettes, so the kid with the pack of whatever brand would share. At that time, the canteen storekeeper would sell cigarettes to the children of adult smokers, thinking we were buying the pack under directions of a parent.

About dinnertime, I would go home to our apartment, on the second floor of #64 building. I would turn on the radio and listen to kids programs like "Tom Mix," "Superman," or "The Green Hornet." These programs were usually over about six in the evening, and it would be time for the evening news. I didn't like listening to the news, so I would put my brother's records on the phonograph to fill the empty space of loneliness.

After fixing my own dinner and eating alone, I'd retire to my bedroom and draw pictures or do a handicraft of some sort, like leatherwork.

During the summer of 1947 I had finally learned to read. I may have known how before, however, it was during that time that I began to look at my dad's "Life" magazines and read the captions and eventually the paragraphs around the pictures. I was so pleased. It was an amazing experience that many take for granted. Reading opens a whole new world to the reader.

During the school semester, I would go to bed about ten o'clock in the evening and fall asleep listing to "I Love a Mystery" centered around characters, Jack, Doc and Reggie. If Pop was working, he'd get home after I went to sleep. He might be asleep when I left for school the following morning. We could go for days without seeing each other. I was learning to be my own parent.

THE BENCH

It was late in the summer of 1948. Again, summer school had been great fun. I had been in the school play at the end of the session. I got to know Marie La Rocca much better and made more friends at Marina Junior High.

My brother, Harold, had returned from the Navy and was planning to attend San Francisco City College. He said he would major in music and wanted to learn to play the tuba.

His sleeping place was in the same hallway Pop's bed was in. A curtain hung between the two beds and the dressers were placed back to back as a second barrier.

Evening meals were more fun with Harold there almost every evening. Harold made sure we had a greater variety of foods to eat. The Navy had allowed him to experience a wider variety of foods.

Several times in the late summer Harold took me to town to Sherman and Clay to buy more records for his collection. He added several Souza marches so he could hear the part of the bass player.

ALCATRAZ: My Home Town

Some time in the fall of that year, Pop, Harold and I had moved to a new apartment, on the North East corner of the first balcony of the old #64 Bldg. Bobby was coming back from Douglas, where he had been living with Her.

The new apartment allowed Harold and Bobby to have a bedroom with twin beds, while Pop had the largest bedroom with the big double bed. My room was an oversized closet, across the hall from the boys' room. I had a single bed on a wire frame without the wooden headboard. I had made a square hole in the sheetrock for my radio. I also had a hanging wall lamp, so I could read and do artwork while sitting on my bed.

Near the end of August, a new boy showed up on the big parade ground. He was a head taller than me and wore brown corduroy slacks, not in style in our area. He had dark, wavy hair and smiled back quickly when I greeted him. He was bouncing a basketball and would run, while dribbling, then would use both hands to aim the ball at the basket. The basket was on the outside wall of the big yellow building near the middle of the big parade ground. The shoes he was wearing were hard brown leather with thick soles and they covered large feet.

He threw the ball toward me. I caught it and dribbled toward the basket and shot. We played for quite awhile before stopping to rest on the bench near the northwest side of the parade ground.

He said his name was Robert Ledwith. We talked about when he had come to the island and where he was living now. I asked him about what grade he was in. He was in the eighth grade, a grade ahead of me.

The workingwomen were coming up the stairs from the dock. That meant it was about 5:30 PM. Time for me to go home and Robert had to get home, too. He said he needed to help his mother fix dinner.

Over the next couple of weeks, we got to play basketball almost daily. As the days went by, several of the other teens joined us and at times we even had enough people to play a real game.

When school started, on the first Tuesday after Labor Day, Robert was on the early morning boat with the rest of the junior high school aged kids. He was nice and mixed well with the rest of the teens.

On a midweek morning in November, we had all decided to walk up Van Ness Avenue to Chestnut Street to get to school. The group included Eddie, Joe, Janet, Myrna, Robert and me. About half way up Chestnut, Janet and I spotted pieces of a letter, still in the envelope, that had been torn to pieces, lying on the sidewalk. We picked up all the pieces and carefully removed the green paper pieces. It became apparent that the green paper was a torn five-dollar bill. We formed a huddle and decided to meet after school, near the donut shop at the corner of Fillmore and Chestnut streets.

After school, I told the group I'd take the money into the bank and get a whole five-dollar bill. Inside

ALCATRAZ: My Home Town

the bank, the teller helped me tape the pieces of green paper together. When it was made whole, she handed me a nice five-dollar bill. I was walking on a cloud when I emerged from the bank.

View of the prison from #64 Building

We went across the street to the donut shop and bought five dollars worth of glazed donuts. We shared them with everyone present, and yet it still seemed like a lot of glazed donuts to eat.

Dinner came too early for all of us on that day.

One evening, before Thanksgiving, I was babysitting for a tiny diaper baby, in "A" building. Just after I had bottle-fed the babe and gotten him to sleep, there was a soft knock on the door. When I opened the door, Robert was standing there. He said he had finished practicing his violin and could visit for a while. His parents had gone to town on the last boat and would not be home until about seven-thirty.

We settled onto the couch and began to hug, then kiss. It was then that I felt something on my left breast. It was his right hand!

"Oh no! I don't want you to do that." I said to him. He seemed surprised.

Soon after that, while reassuring him that I still liked him, I walked him out the door and said goodnight.

In early December, Robert asked me to the Christmas Formal, put on by the Women's Club. I accepted his invitation with glee.

The challenge now was for me to get a formal gown. Pop was the one in charge of where to buy it and how much money to spend. He got one of his lady friends to go with us to Grayson's Department store, on Mission Street.

My breasts were large and developed. I wore a thirty-six, "D" cup bra. I had learned that having big boobs caused some people to think I had sexual experience to match my bra size. For that reason, I wanted a dress that would down play my boobs. I picked a light blue, full dress with puffy short sleeves. Looking back at pictures of that dress today, I can't tell you how ugly it was.

Christmas formal: I'm the first one the right, bottom row. Robert Ledwith is directly behind me

The other things I had to have for the formal dance included a girdle to hold up my nylons and a pair of dancing shoes. The saleswoman at Grayson's was very helpful. She was able to sell me a half-slip to wear under the formal dress.

The Christmas formal was on a Saturday evening. That gave me the morning to put my hair up in pin curls.

On the Saturday evening of the dance, I got dressed in all my new clothes. The girdle was a real challenge to get on. The next test was to hook the nylon stockings to the garter snaps on the girdle. This skill never got well developed.

Robert was there to pick me up right on time. He was dressed in dark slacks, a dress shirt with a tie, and a sports jacket with matching light colored sleeves and collar, and dark vest-like body. He was the only boy at the dance not wearing a suit.

Marvin Orr, Betty and Bobby's dad, had decorated the Social Hall. He had a very special talent with crepe paper. The hall became a wonderland.

The music was played over a PA system and was mostly waltzes or fox trots. We had a wonderful time. The Women's Club had made punch, which was served in fancy crystal cups. There were also little sandwiches; cut into bite sized triangles, some deviled eggs, small sweet pickles and dark olives to snack on.

Over forty-five teens were present at the dance. About half of the attendees were kids from the city. They were visiting the island for the first time, because one of the island residents had invited them to the dance.

To be on the island for this occasion, a resident had to invite the visitor and notify the dock officer a week ahead of time. The boat officer was then to allow the visitor onto the boat for the ride from the city to the island. Once on the island, each visitor had to sign into the "Visitor Register." Many of the visitors on this evening were for the high school kids attending the Christmas Formal.

No one was allowed to wander beyond the Social Hall, where the dance was being held.

We all danced a lot. Few stood on the sidelines to watch. Our adult chaperones were a couple of young officers and their wives, dressed in their best "Sunday go to meeting" clothes. If a young couple were thought to be dancing too close to each other, a chaperone would tap the shoulder of the boy and ask that several inches of light be seen between the two bodies. The teens co-operated, knowing that defiance of the rule would result in them being asked to leave the party.

The dance ended in time for the city kids to catch the ten o'clock boat back to the city. The last song played was "Good Night Ladies." Robert and I went back to my place in #64 Building, where he walked me to my door and kissed me "good night." I went into my living room, where Pop was waiting for me. He wanted to know if I had had a good time. We talked for quite awhile about all the things I had observed at the dance.

Christmas came soon after the formal dance. The story of the birth of Jesus in the manger, with the shepherds, the wise men and the angels who sang on high was produced for a large audience. Then our choir sang carols.

As we finished the last carol, the sound of jingle bells could be heard throughout the auditorium.

Santa Claus came into the hall. Chairs were moved to make a place for his throne and for the bags of Christmas candy his elves would hand to the children as they got off of Santa's lap. Most of the junior high kids went to see Santa. No one wanted to miss the candy.

It was almost Spring Break when our group began to spend Friday and Saturday evenings out on the bench, on the east side of the island. The view was spectacular! We could see all the lights from the oil refinery near Richmond, across the San Francisco Bay Bridge and over to Powell Street in the city.

Robert and I were there one evening, after dark. He and I were sitting on the bench with a group of friends, who were standing facing us while talking and smoking. Over the chatter and laughter, suddenly we heard Robert's mother calling in her whiney voice, "Robert, are you out there?"

His parents had forbidden Robert from going to the bench. Apparently, they had heard that it was a place where young people met to get close to each other.

By the second time she called his name, both he and I had jumped to the left side of the rising where the bench was and had hidden behind the plants and large cactus, out of sight of the bench area. We could hear the metal gate open and knew she was just above us at the bench.

Now she called out in a louder voice, "Robert, are you there?"

Silence.

Then we heard, "Oh Dear! I'm having a heart attack. Oh, my heart! My heart!" she said almost breathlessly.

Robert couldn't handle it any more, so he got out of hiding and went up the path to the bench and talked quietly to his mother. They left the area together.

They had been gone a while before the rest of us came out of hiding and continued our conversations and smoking.

Within the next week, Robert's parents had him enrolled in California Concordia College, a private Lutheran boarding school, in Oakland. He was allowed to come home every other weekend. He and I wrote letters to each other for several months, and then we lost contact.

He and his family left Alcatraz in the summer months of 1950. We had lost contact with each other by then. There are people and events that I have forgotten about Alcatraz, but I do remember Robert.

TEEN SOCIAL LIFE

In the fall of 1948, I was in the eighth grade at Marina Junior High School at Fillmore and Bay streets in San Francisco and my family still lived on Alcatraz Island, in the old #64 Building, on the first balcony at the east end.

Our age group had begun to grow closer as we approached the onset of puberty. We now arranged meetings to play games at our friends' homes or show up at an apartment when the parents were off the island for the evening to dance, or talk about the mysteries of the adult world.

We also spent more time in San Francisco going to movies, spending summer days at Play Land at the beach, and riding on streetcars, trolley cars and buses.

As a group, we pretended it was important to have "forbidden" objects on the walls of our bedrooms. It became a challenge to steal the municipal bus number from the case at the back window. The bus we rode most often was the #19 Polk Street. Our group would stand in the aisle of the bus, as though getting ready to leave by the back door. When the driver could not see the right side of the back seat, a member of our group would simply slide the number, printed on a thin piece of 10" by 10" wood, out of it's metal frame and hide it under a jacket until he or she was off the bus.

I had the #19 plaque on the wall of my bedroom. My brother Bobby had a pair of girls' panties stapled on his bedroom wall.

The handball court was inside the ugly two-story high light-yellow sideboard building in the middle of the big parade ground, near the fence separating the prison from the residence. The sand box and swings were on the south side of the building. The basketball hoop was hung on the north-facing wall.

The adults on Alcatraz were more aware than we realized of our behavior. One of the very caring adults, Lt. Phil Bergen, took special interest to keep us involved in constructive physical activity.

He opened the door to the handball court and set up a volleyball court for us. He encouraged us to separate into teams and compete with each other. He made sure the place was open two evenings a week for teenagers.

After several months, he set up a Ping-Pong table in the top level of the handball court, which overlooked the main floor, so we could have regular competitions. Most of us played Ping-Pong. I was very good at it, however, Donnie Hurley was the best and I got tired of being beaten by him. Not many girls played, even though it was great fun.

Marjorie Manderville was in the same age group as my big brother Harold. She had gone to school with that group and graduated from one of the high schools in San Francisco.

After graduation from high school, Marjorie joined the San Francisco ballet company. When she married Warren Hack, the prison medical officer, she gave up the ballet. In the early fall of 1948, she decided to teach several classes of dance to the girls of Alcatraz.

The teen girls met once a week, in the solarium on the fourth floor of "C" Building. The dancers included Betty Lou Orr, Betty Hart, Agnes Roberts, Kay Bergen, Margaret and me. There were more, however, I have forgotten their names.

The elementary age girls met on a different day and the really little girls on yet another day. My little sister was not interested in taking dance lessons.

Before Christmas, Marjorie had us dancing to classical music and helped us get knee-length tutus, in white gauze-like material. The dance costumes were sewn by one of the mothers. We each paid for the cost of the material. With our white leather dance slippers, we looked like the real thing!

Dancing to "Moon Light Sonata", we were one of the hits of the Christmas program. The younger kids were so cute the audience made a lot of "ooh" and "aah" sounds.

ALCATRAZ: My Home Town

Betty Orr really wanted to continue on and become a ballerina. When, after high school, she began to take dance from an instructor in San Francisco, she learned that she would be unable to ever stand on her toes because of some sort of injury to her right foot.

Some of the island kids were not allowed to play with us when we were in elementary school. Several of the parents thought of us as too rough and unmannered. Now they came when we got together on the parade ground, in the gymnasium, or at house parties.

Joe Burdett was one of those kids.

He had come to Alcatraz from McNeil Island, Washington. He lived on the first floor, east end of "B" building. From the parade ground, we could often see him watching us through the glass door of his dining area. His mother was one of the workingwomen, who left the island daily to go to a job in San Francisco.

Joe walked to school with us and was a part of the group then. I did not understand why he didn't come out to play in the early years. It was years later that he explained the rationale of his parents.

At the junior high school, a talent assembly was put on to allow kids to show their accomplishments. A truly gifted ballerina was to perform. To help her appearance, a teacher asked for three volunteers to appear with her. I volunteered.

The gifted gal showed the other three of us how to move and how to pose to the music. The white tutu from the Christmas dance was just right! At the time of the talent assembly, the dance stage was flooded with blue lights and the prima ballerina with her toe slippers occupied the attention of the crowd. In the background the three of us did a ballet walk in time to the music, then posed in a ballet form. The dance lasted less than five minutes. The applause lasted almost as long as the dance. Many in the crowd had never seen ballet dancing before. The audience was astounded!

In the New Year, 1949, our dance instructor, Marjorie made arrangements for a large group of Alcatraz teens to entertain at Sonoma State Hospital for the Severely Mentally Retarded.

ALCATRAZ: My Home Town

Billy Hart with others at the soda fountain.

Below the dance floor of the Social Hall were two bowling allies where I set pins for .25 cents a game.

There were also 2 pool tables and a small soda fountain.

It took three cars to haul us all up to Sonoma. We were asked to visit with the children in one of the buildings before we went to the hospital auditorium. The children we visited were out in the fenced yard of the building they lived in. The visit was very short. Prior to that time, I don't think any of us had thought about disabled children, except those afflicted with polio.

So they could go to Sonoma with us, Bud Hart, Donnie Hurley, Donnie Martin and Bobby Orr formed a barbershop quartette called "Four Music Keepers." They sang some songs from the pop charts of our parents, like "Sweet Adeline", "Don't Sit Under the Apple Tree", and "When Johnny Comes Marching Home." They sounded very good.

ALCATRAZ: My Home Town

Don Martin (pictured), Bud Hart, Don Hurley and Bobbie Orr sang at Sonoma State Hospital. I mimed to "I Saw Mama Kissing Santa Claus." My costume was the very best pair of pajamas I ever owned. The ballerinas performed to Moon Light Sonata. Robert Ledwith, my first "steady" boyfriend, played a violin solo.

Dressed in the jeans and shirts we came in my friend, Nancy, from school in San Francisco, and I sang a couple of country music duets.

I don't remember the other acts. The whole program was about forty-five minutes long. When it was all over, the members of the cast threw wrapped Double Bubble Gum out to the members of the audience. They were clapping and grabbing the bubble gum. Some needed help to unwrap it before putting it into their mouths. Soon after the excitement of the bubble gum, the children were lined up by the hospital aides and left through the doors at the back of the auditorium.

All in all, it was a great experience. None of us had ever known children as disabled as these children. The experience gave us a lot to think about.

We all got back into the car we had arrived in. On the way back to Pier 4, from the Bay Bridge, we dropped my friend, Nancy, off near Market Street, so she could catch the streetcar home.

As winter passed, the teen girls had a slumber party one Saturday evening, at Kay Bergen's place, the two-story duplex on the east end of the big parade ground. We each took something for the group to munch on and once we arrived at the hosts' house, we dressed in our best pajamas. We lay in a circle, on mats on the living room carpet. For convenience, the food was placed in the center of the circle. Food included Hershey Kisses, potato salad, potato chips, packaged cookies and soda pop, among other stuff.

These years were a time of trying new things. We talked about "petting", a sexual behavior, which started with the guy touching the breast of the girl he was with. Those who had done it reported not knowing why such a big deal was made of it, since it offered not much satisfaction, either to the girl with the breast or to the guy who was doing the massaging.

We talked and giggled most of the night. Several times during the night, a parent, from some other room, would yell at us to "Shut up and go to sleep!" It was to no avail. We'd tone it down to a whisper for a while, and then the sound would gradually go up.

We talked "girl talk" about breast development, pubic hair, underarm hair, and Kotex versus tampons. The girls seemed surprised that I preferred tampons, as many believed that virgins could not wear tampons.

I was still swimming at the Crystal Plunge, in the North Beach area, several times a month. Tampons certainly worked well on those occasions.

Around six in the morning, we decided it would be fun to go to Mass at St. Brigid Church. Some of the girls were too tired, but about six of us put our stylish long coats on over our pajamas. We then rolled up the legs of the pajama bottoms, so they wouldn't show under the coat. We left on the 6:20 boat from Alcatraz. We arrived at Pier 4 at six thirty and walked up the Van Ness Avenue hill to St. Brigid. We were all wearing bandanas at that time. They were in style.

Freeman

Kay Bergan lived in the 2-story duplex.
Her dad was captain, then Associate Warden

ALCATRAZ: My Home Town

Only half the girls were Catholic. It didn't matter. We just followed Agnes and Kay into the main church and when either dipped her fingers into the "Holy Water" or made the signs of the Cross, we mimicked the move. When one of them knelt, we knelt in the same place.

Because we had been eating all night, none of the Catholic girls could take communion. The mass was relatively short and when it was over, we followed our Catholic friends out of the church. We then walked down Van Ness Avenue to Pier 4 and took the morning launch back to Alcatraz.

We all went back to Kay's place to help clean up our mess and get our belongings before going home to catch some sleep.

When a mother, on Alcatraz, had trouble talking to her daughter about developmental changes, the rest of us would fill in the necessary information or misinformation.

It was about that time that "Very Personally Yours" was shown in the junior high school girls' gym classes. It was a movie about development and menstruation that Kotex Company and Walt Disney produced. When the movie was over, we knew what we needed to know about the how and why of Kotex and sanitary belts. We had learned nothing about making babies.

The canteen, on Alcatraz, was right across from the Post Office. The hours were similar. Both were closed in the afternoon from noon until three o'clock.

The stock in the canteen was limited, much like the canteens on military bases few fresh vegetables were offered and most of the canned goods were off brands.

The Kotex boxes were wrapped in plain brown paper. Still, everyone knew what you were buying when you bought it. It sat on the highest shelf, right next to another box in a plain brown wrapper, which contained Tampax.

If the clerk was a man, I'd wait till later when his wife was there to buy sanitary supplies. Because of the size of the island, some of the people in the canteen kept track of who was buying supplies and who wasn't. Sometimes we would hear gossip about the women who missed their periods or more to the point, hadn't bought sanitary supplies for several months.

When our young women got married on short notice, the people who ran the canteen would be in on how soon to expect a baby in that new family.

A LARGER WORLD

Spring was on the way. School would be out for Easter Vacation. Public schools and Catholic schools had slightly different days off.

On the weekend before vacation, Kay Bergen invited me to go with her, her father, Bobby Orr, Mr. Orr and Bud Hart on a camping trip. I really wanted to go, but I had to be sure that the rest of my family would look after my little sister, Betty. After a talk with Pop, I was able to joyfully tell Kay, "Yes!"

On the day were we leaving, just as with the stay at the Stites' farm, I piled my clothing into a pillowcase. I rolled up my mummy sleeping bag very tightly, so it wouldn't take too much space. We all met on the Alcatraz dock for an early morning boat.

Bobby was small, so he had to ride in the front seat. He was between his dad, Marvin Orr, and Lt. Bergen, who was driving. Bud Hart had to sit with Kay and me in the back seat. We had no idea where we were going, we just knew it was going to be fun.

At first the scenery was familiar. Bay Street toward the Bay Bridge, then through the toll booth toward Oakland, then a right hand turn through new city areas where we had not been before. After a long time, we were driving through small towns, and then we began passing miles of newly plowed fields with curly ribbons of dark brown moving away from the highway for miles and miles. Then the scenery turned to sand dunes and miles of emptiness.

We stopped by the roadside to make a simple lunch of peanut butter and jelly sandwiches. At the next filling station, we used the bathroom and got a drink of water.

The sun was behind the mountains on the west when we passed by the sign, which read "Death Valley." The road became very narrow. Had a car come from the other direction, our car might need to pull off the road to the right a little. There was no white line down the middle.

Lt. Bergen stopped in front of the Park Ranger's office. He and Mr. Orr went inside, while all of us kids got out of the car and walked around. It felt good to get off our butts.

It was hotter here than it ever had been in Douglas, Arizona, where I came from, and it wasn't even Easter yet!

When the men came out of the Ranger's office, we were told that we would be spending the night in a camping area of Death Valley.

We all got back into the car. As the car pulled away from the Ranger Station, we made sure the windows were all the way down, so the air would blow the sweat off our faces. By this time, Bobby and Bud had changed seats several times. When we got to the special place, there was a large marker stating something to the effect that "this place is the lowest place in California." Lt. Bergen explained that this area was well below the level of the sea or San Francisco Bay.

We drove on as the sun, setting behind the hills, made great dark shadows on the road.

We reached a place by the side of the road where it was decided that we should spend the night. We unpacked only the minimum of stuff. Sleeping bags and blanket rolls were put in one stack. Then the men got out the food box and the water container. We were all encouraged to drink water. It seemed it had been a very long time since the last drink. The thirst was almost desperate.

Lt. Bergen gave toilet instructions. He explained that if we only had to pee, we could do that anywhere out of sight of the group. If we had to poop, however, we were to get the little hand shovel, go where we could not be seen. Then we needed to dig a hole for the poop. Poop into the hole, then cover the poop with the dirt removed from the hole. I was so happy to be constipated.

We all helped fix the baloney sandwiches for dinner. There was no water for washing dishes, so the dinner had to be something that required no dishes. By the time we finished eating, the sun had gone down and it was very dark. There was no moon to see in the sky. The heat of the day went away quickly and it turned almost cold.

We got our sleeping bags laid out, and after taking care of the necessary toileting, we each crawled into our own sleeping bag. The stars seemed much brighter in that desert sky than in the sky over the cities of the bay. Sleep came easily.

The following morning, when I woke, I could not open my eyes. When I checked them with my fingers, they were filled with sand from the desert. I had to sit up and turn my head over the dirt to drop those fine grains of sand from my eyes.

We had dry cereal for breakfast, and then packed the car, got a big drink of water and Lt. Bergen drove toward the exit from Death Valley. There were no green plants anywhere along the roads. No birds flying overhead. No rabbits were seen along the side of the road. No signs of life at all.

The men checked in at the Ranger Station to let them know that we were leaving the park.

Just outside Death Valley, the road began to climb up some mountains. At the first gas station, we all got to use a real toilet and wash our hands and faces with running water.

The scenery going up the mountain road was pretty. There was not much traffic. The signs announced that Las Vegas was east on highway 95. The higher up the mountain we rode, the cooler the weather became. It was nice to feel the cool air.

We began to sing old barber shop music with harmonies. You might remember "Me and My Gal," "When you wore a Tulip," and "When Johnny Comes Marching Home."

Before we reached Las Vegas, the car turned onto US Highway 15 toward Lake Mead. This highway was wider. There were places to pull off the road to allow the cars behind to go ahead. Lt. Bergen didn't ever pull off the road. There were not often cars behind us.

It was only a little past noon when we drove by the Ranger Station at Lake Mead. When Lt. Bergen pulled over to get the camping permit from the ranger, we all got out of the car to stretch our legs. It felt so good to have my feet on solid ground. There were very tall green trees all about. Some of the trees had blossoms in them.

The camping permit was put on the inside of the front windshield. We all got back into the car and the men began to look for a good place to camp.

There were several areas where we could see a public outhouse. The men talked about finding a place close to an outhouse and a short distance from the lake so we could swim during the day.

The place they finally settled on was about a block from the edge of the lake and about the same distance from a public outhouse.

We unpacked the car. The food was placed near the fire pit. Kay and I went to the outhouse to change into our bathing suits. We headed right for the lake.

Once we got into the water, it was obvious that this lake water is different than the water in the swimming pools in San Francisco. This water didn't taste salty and more effort was required to float. Lake Mead is a fresh water lake!

After swimming for a while, we got out and lay on our towels on the beach. The boys came down to the water after a time and we all went back into the water.

We heard a shrill whistle from the camping area. That was the call to come back to camp to help fix dinner. Stew was the evening meal. We sopped up the juice with bread.

All the kids helped with the cleanup while the men enjoyed an after dinner beer.

As the sun was going down, the men built a campfire up to light the area and to make it warmer. We sat around the campfire and sang songs in harmony. Several hours after dinner, the men cut switches from a nearby bush. The thin end of each switch was cut to a point so we could roast marshmallows. Several times, the marshmallow would catch on fire. The fire had to be blown out or the whole thing would turn into black charcoal.

We were all tired after a wonderful day. The girls got to go to the outhouse first. The boys were nearby when we came out.

It felt so good to get into the sleeping bag. There was a little bit of sand in my bag. That didn't keep me from sleeping. Again, the stars were so much brighter, away from the lights of the city.

When we woke the following morning, Lt. Bergen reminded us that it was Easter morning. The day was planned out for us. We would have breakfast, then, we would take care of any bathroom needs, clean up the camp area, pack up our stuff and go into Boulder City for Easter morning Mass.

We finished breakfast, washed, dried and packed the dishes and food away for the trip back to San Francisco. Then Lt. Bergen put a pot of water on the campfire, so we could wash with warm water and a washcloth to clean up a bit. None of us had any "Sunday go to meeting clothes."

On this morning, we each went to the outhouse alone with our pillow- case of clean clothing. While there we dressed in the cleanest clothing we had. While visiting the outhouse, we each dressed in the cleanest clothing we had. The stuff we had brought with us were "play clothes."

One by one we returned to the campsite to clean and pack things away for the trip home by way of Boulder City.

Lt. Bergen and Mr. Orr lifted the boxes and packed them in the trunk of the car. On top of the boxes went the bedrolls and sleeping bags. There was more room back there now than when we first started on this outing.

Lt. Bergen reminded us that the site should "look better than we found it." When we finished the clean up, it did.

Kay and I piled into the back seat of the car with Bud Hart. Bobby got in the middle of the front seat. Lt. Bergen drove and Mr. Orr sat in the front passenger side where he could smoke without the smoke bothering anyone. We drove out of the Lake Mead Recreational area and onto the highway that would carry us over Boulder Dam. It seemed to take very little time before we were driving over the top of Boulder Dam and looking at Lake Mead on the right side of the dam and the great deep Grand Canyon out the window on the left.

Lt. Bergen talked about the electrical power made by the water pouring through the dam and turning the turbines. He said that the dam made electricity for many of the states in the West. At that time, I was too young to be aware of the significance of his statements.

Lt. Bergen parked the car in a turnout along the roadway so we could get out and look down at the Grand Canyon. Looking back, we were all impressed with the depth of the dam.

Back in the car and headed for Boulder City for Easter Sunday mass we were rather quiet. We knew this wonderful trip would be over at the end of the day and we would be back in school on Monday.

The road was mountainous with curves and pullouts for really slow drivers. When we passed the sign announcing Boulder City Limits, Lt. Bergen pulled off and opened his road map. He studied it for a moment, and then seemed to know just where to go.

I could see the church steeples before we got close enough to park. The sign outside read "St Andrews Catholic Church".

Years later I would learn that St Andrews Catholic Church is one of the oldest churches in Boulder City. It was built about the time the construction workers arrived to build the dam.

Lt. Bergen parked the car in a dirt parking lot, across the street from the church. It was almost ten o'clock on Easter morning. We were going to attend a very long Mass.

Neither Kay nor I had head covering. Lt. Bergen gave Kay his pocket-handkerchief to cover her head. A woman I had never seen before in my life, overhearing our conversation, handed me her bandana and assured me she had more at home.

Just as before, I followed Kay and mimicked her every move. When she dipped her fingers in the holy water, I dipped my fingers in the holy water, when she would kneel down, I would kneel down, when she made the sign of the cross, I made the sign of the cross.

Kay walked up to a pew near the altar. She kneeled, and then entered the pew. I followed. Bobby and Bud were close behind us in the same pew, then Mr. Orr and Lt. Bergen. It was a very long

Mass. Most of the service was in Latin. The music was beautiful. I remember it from my brother Harold's, classic music collection. It was the "Hallelujah Chorus."

The priest talked about each of the statues in the church. Each statue represented one of the Stations of the Cross, events that occurred on the day Jesus was crucified. We heard of the condemnation to death, Jesus being forced to carry the heavy cross, and about Jesus falling the first time. The priest continued to the place on the road where Jesus met his mother, then when Simon helped Jesus carry the cross. At each station of the cross, the priest talked about what each of us should learn about helping people who are struggling.

Near the end of his sermon, the priest talked of Jesus being laid in the tomb and the rock being rolled in front of it.

He then spoke of the miracle of Easter and why we celebrate.

The time we took to go to Mass was well spent.

We piled into the car and before noon, Lt. Bergen was turning the car toward home. After several hours, we turned onto Highway 99 headed north. It was about this time that the men decided to stop by the roadside to fix sandwiches for lunch. As before, we all made our own sandwich, using the peanut butter and jelly on the sliced white bread. We had water to wash it down.

At the next gas station, on 99 north, Lt. Bergen pulled in to get the tank filled. We all took that opportunity to use the restrooms.

The trip to San Francisco took almost ten hours. The fields were familiar. The farmers were plowing and planting as we passed them. Now and then we had to slow for a piece of farm equipment, on the highway, being moved from one field to another. Farmhouses were few and far between. The car moved from the farm fields to small settlements of houses, then larger towns like Fresno or Modesto.

We amused ourselves on the long ride by singing, playing "hangman" or sleeping. Mr. Orr and Lt. Bergen took turns behind the wheel. About every two hours we'd stop so everyone could get out of the car and stretch their legs.

We stopped for an evening meal near Fresno. Sandwiches again. One nice thing about being home would be, not having sandwiches for lunch and dinner.

Just outside Stockton, we stopped one last time for gas and restrooms.

It was getting dark. The sun had set and reflective colors bounced off the clouds. The views became more filled with lights and buildings and the buildings became taller and wider. There were traffic lights along this part of the highway. Soon we were going through Oakland. The area was now familiar as we approached the Bay Bridge.

ALCATRAZ: My Home Town

The traffic was light at this time of night. We could see our hometown sitting in the middle of the bay with the lighthouse flashing brightly in a rhythm, as it continued its circular motion around the whole of San Francisco Bay. We went through the tunnel on Treasure Island and out on the other side where the Ferry Building seemed close enough to reach out and touch.

The car turned onto Bay Street. Now we were all wide-awake. Just a few minutes and we would drive onto Pier 4, unpack the back of the car, check to be sure we got all our possessions out of the car seats and left the inside of the car clean.

All of us kids stayed outside on the dock. It was so good to smell the salt air, feel the chill in the breeze and see the bright lights of our city.

Soon we could see the Warden Johnson rounding the east side of the Island heading our way. In no time at all we would all be home getting ready for bed so we could get up in the morning and go to school.

What a wonderful trip it was. We were all left with great memories. Now it's just nice to be home.

NEW FRIENDS

Alcatraz, as with most federal prisons, had a regular turnover of personnel. As some of our friends moved to other places, new friends arrived with their families.

In 1949, my eighth-grade year, Joy and Darleen Stucker, Brian, Tom and Allen Severson were among the newcomers. Joy, Brian and Tom were all in our age group and joined us in most of our activities. Darleen and Allen hung out with the high school or early college aged group.

On our walks to school that year, it became obvious that Joe Burdette and Joy were getting very friendly with each other and soon they began to go steady. The young romantics made the walk to and from school more fun. They would hold hands and try to keep people from seeing what they were doing.

Just as most teenagers become interested in music and dancing, my friends on Alcatraz began listening to popular music stations on their radios.

I don't remember the call letters of the stations, but I had four that I listened to. One was for popular

ALCATRAZ: My Home Town

music played by the big bands. The second was a twenty-four-hour country music station. Country music was often where we heard the first strains of what would turn into the top of the "Pop Charts." I had a classical music station that played the music without the lyrics. Saturday and Sunday morning I wanted to hear the weekend melodramas and serial stories, which were entertaining.

I didn't have to buy records. My brother, Harold, let me use his. He trusted me to be very careful with them.

We all looked forward to Friday or Saturday evenings. Some of our parents went off the island with friends to enjoy an evening in San Francisco at one of the bars on North Beach or at a movie theater.

I stepped out of our apartment, on the first balcony of #64 Building and watched the people getting on the seven o'clock boat on weekend evenings. Soon after the boat left the island, I was on my way to my friend's house. The parents were out for the evening. In little time, word got around and members of our group began to show up.

Sometimes, we brought refreshments, like a six-pack of Coke or cup cakes, which could be purchased at the canteen. I always took cigarettes to share with others. Because Pop had let me smoke at home since I was in fifth grade, I could be counted on to bring cigarettes. Several of my young friends were also smokers. We just didn't do the smoking in public places.

Once the group got together, music was the next item on the agenda. Phonographs were common. We could put our favorite records on to play, then pick a partner and dance. We dimmed the lights and danced, often on the living room carpet.

Some of those songs I remember to this day. Remember "You're Breaking My Heart," "Someday You'll Want Me to Want You," "She Wore a Yellow Ribbon," or that silly song "I've Got a Lovely Bunch of Coconuts"

Joe Burdette Jr. threw a surprise
birthday party for his girlfriend, Joy Stucker

ALCATRAZ: My Home Town

Now and then one of our friends would bring some alcohol, smuggled from home. We mixed the booze with Coke or some other soft drink before consuming it.

About ten in the evening, we'd be very aware of the time. We joined together and cleaned up the area we had been partying in, till it looked better than when the parents left. About ten fifteen we'd send someone to the top balcony of old # 64 Building so they could see who got off the boat. If the parents got off the boat, the phone would ring. Our friend would answer the phone to learn whether to send people home or not.

Generally, most of us were expected to be home by eleven in the evening on weekends. Because it was such a close community, many parents were less concerned than they should have been, about their kids.

This year, Joe Burdett was really involved with our group. Because Joe was going steady with Joy, he decided to throw a surprise birthday party for her. His mother helped him plan it. She got the birthday cake and the other party refreshments. It was Joe's job to take each of us aside, one at a time, to tell us the where and when of the party. He also tried to get us to get her presents that he knew she would like. He knew which records she wanted, and what her favorite color was, in case we bought a sweater.

Joy was very bright. In a short time, she was sure we were all talking about her behind her back and her feelings were very hurt. When she confronted Joe about all the whispering behind her back, he had to confess about the surprise party. He then made her promise to "act surprised." She did. A wonderful time was had by all.

It was in the spring of any year that we stood on the balcony as some of the dads returned from a prison train trip to drop off and pick up prisoners from other federal prisons in the United States. We had heard that one of the prisoners they were bringing back was the killer from the State of Nevada, who had thrown his victims into a well.

The "chain" usually had a lead Federal Prison Officer, in full uniform, with his wrist chained to the wrist of the prisoner behind him. That prisoner had his ankles chained with just enough room on the chain length to allow him to take short steps. There was a length of chain between his hands another prisoner was chained to him, with both hands and ankles connected. Some times there would be as many as five individuals chained together. An officer would be in the front and in the back of the chain.

The "chain" had two purposes. The first was to take inmates from Alcatraz, who had almost finished their federal prison time, to a prison closer to their discharge point or near the place where they had been imprisoned in the first place. Sometimes a prisoner was headed for Springfield, Illinois, which was the psychiatric prison for crazy prisoners. The second purpose was to pick up prisoners from prisons, where they had proven to be escape risks.

The best thought about the event was that the dads would be home after being away, sometimes for as long as two weeks. As we stood there watching, we knew the prisoners were in jail for killing, or robbing, or other illegal acts.

We knew these bad guys needed to be controlled.

ROOM FOR ONE MORE

Spring of 1948 brought Her to Vallejo. This time, apparently, She had a plan to stay. She had driven my stepfather Zollie's, old Dodge pickup truck. In the bed of the pick up she could pack in boxes. My little sister, Skookie, had ridden in the front seat all the way from Douglas, Arizona. They drove to Grandmother Gibbons' place, in the little town of Vallejo.

Long after this day, I would learn more about the trip and Her plan.

As She would tell me, later that year, She had planned the move with a neighbor in the housing development. They would wait for Zollie to be picked up by a fellow worker, to go on a painting job. After he left the house, She and the neighbor packed everything into boxes and stacked the boxes in the bed of the Dodge. When all the packing was done, She packed a suitcase for herself and another for Skookie. On her way out of Douglas, She dropped by "A" Avenue Elementary School and picked up my six-year-old sister. With my sister in the front seat, She dropped by the bank and emptied the joint account. They left Douglas on their way to California via Bisbee. In Bisbee, She dropped her filing papers for a divorce from Zollie, with her lawyer. She signed the necessary papers and paid the man. Then She left the state.

Skookie had turned six in September of 1947.

Grandmother Gibbons was purposely sick all the time. Her third husband, Walter, worked in the ship yards every weekday, then came home to fix dinner for himself and Grandmother. On his weekends off, he cleaned the house, changed the bed linens and helped her out to the back yard.

He had built a special wooden elevator that allowed Grandmother to sit in a chair, just outside the back door. He would then let the wooden frame lower gradually to the ground by controlling a handle unwinding rope from a roller. After the four-foot ride, she could stand and walk, ever so slowly, around the back yard. When she tired of the scenery, she would sit in the chair and he would crank the handle, winding up the lift rope to pull the elevator up to the level of the back door.

It was less than a week before Grandmother Gibbons demanded that Skookie be taken somewhere else to live. "That child just takes too much out of me," she whined.

According to the report I got from Pop, She put Skookie in the front seat of the Dodge with her suitcase. She then drove around the neighborhood for several blocks, looking for children playing in a front yard. When She found the children, She parked the truck in front of the house and took my little sister with her suitcase to the front door. She knocked on the door and talked to the woman who answered. She asked if Skookie could stay there. She promised the woman a weekly "paycheck" for keeping the child. When the woman agreed to keep the child, Skookie was left at the strange house with people she did not know.

Reportedly, She had phoned the Alcatraz armory and left a message for Pop. Soon after that, Pop spent his days off in the city with Her. They stayed at my Aunt Eleanor's place.

When he got home, he told me about my baby sister being left with a stranger. Her leaving the little girl surprised neither him nor me.

ALCATRAZ: My Home Town

I remember, even at thirteen years of age, how angry I felt. "We have to go find her and bring her home." I said to my father.

Me, Pop (dad), and little sister Betty

He did not own a car at that time, so he had to call one of the other officers and ask to borrow one. As soon as he got the car keys, he and I left on the next boat. We found the car parked at the bottom of Van Ness Avenue, near Pier 4. We got in and headed over the Bay Bridge, past Berkeley and on to Vallejo. Soon after arriving in Vallejo, we saw the giant Barrel Club and turned right on that street.

Pop knew the way to Grandmother Gibbons from there. When we passed the Gibbon's house, we went up and down several streets until we came to the yard where children were playing outside. Sure enough, there was Skookie.

Pop let me out. I walked up to the house and knocked on the door. I explained to the woman who answered that I was Skookie's big sister, and that her father and I had come to pick her up to take her to live with us. Without much question, the woman got Skookie's suitcase for me, and then Skookie and I got in the back seat of the borrowed car. Pop drove us back to the city and to a parking place on the lower part of Van Ness Avenue.

We all caught the boat home. I don't know when Pop told Her that he and I had Skookie.

When we arrived on the island, Pop and I had to go into the left side of the dock office to sign Skookie in. At that time, Pop made arrangements for Skookie to get a resident card for living on Alcatraz.

As soon as we got to our apartment in #64 Bldg., Skookie and I unpacked her suitcase. I had to rearrange my clothing in the chest of drawers so her clothing would fit in the bottom two drawers.

Then it was bath time. Skookie had never lived in a place with a bathtub. I showed her how to adjust the bath water and stayed with her for awhile as she bathed.

Her hair was dark brown and about shoulder length. Her frame was tall and slender, even for a six-year-old. I laid out fresh P. J. s for her, then helped her dry. She didn't need my help. I just didn't want her to feel alone.

That night, she slept in my bed with my arms around her. When we got up the following morning, we had breakfast, and then went out to explore the parade grounds and to see if we could find other children her age.

She talked about all the water and the boats around Alcatraz. In Douglas, Arizona the only large body of water is the public swimming pool, in the park.

After finding the parade grounds empty, I took her to the Dolby's apartment on the second balcony, just above our place. Jeanie Dolby was close to Skookie's age. Mrs. Dolby said she would have Jeanie walk Skookie home in about an hour. That gave the girls time to play dolls and to get to know one another.

Pop arranged to have another twin sized bed delivered to our place. It arrived by noon. Skookie and I made the bed. With each bed pushed up against the wall, on each side of the room, there was just enough space for us to walk between the beds.

It didn't take long for her to learn to go to sleep with the light still on so I could study. She fit right into the family, and took on chores assigned by my brother, Harold, as we all did.

On Sunday evening, after I washed her hair in the kitchen sink, we had a discussion about what she wanted her name to be. She had been given the birth name of Tessa Bell Campbell. She did not like the name "Tessa Bell."

As we talked about the options, she said she liked the names Vickie and Betty. I told her she had to choose between the two so I could get her enrolled in school. By morning, at breakfast time, she said she had decided on the name "Betty." She proved to me that she could spell B-e-t-t-y. We were ready for a new day.

Skookie and I joined the other Alcatraz kids on the 7:20 A.M. launch. She and I walked with the others on their way to Marina Junior High School. As the rest of my friends entered the school yard, my little sister and I walked on down Bay Street, then turned left at North Point Street and to the front of Winfield Scott School. There we entered the building and found the principal's office.

I explained to the school secretary that my little sister was there to start in Winfield Scott School as a first grader. Since she had come from Arizona, where education was a year ahead, there was no question about her being ready. The secretary filled out some basic information, on a card, using the name Betty Campbell.

I asked about other children in the school who lived on Alcatraz. The secretary assured me that she would have one of the Alcatraz kids walk to the dock with Betty. Then the secretary handed me a bundle of information cards to be filled out and signed by a parent. She and I walked Betty to her first-grade class room and met her teacher. At that time, I hugged her goodbye and left the school.

When I got back to the junior high school, I dropped by the office and told the girls' vice principal where I had been and why. She wrote me a pass to class and said she would not count this event as a "tardy".

When school was out for the day, I could hardly wait to get to the dock. I needed to know that my little sister had made it to Pier 4 safely.

Not only was she there, she was running and playing with the other kids her age. She had a lovely smile and a happy, easy laugh. She seemed to be doing just fine.

After getting home from school, she would often go to visit friends or go up to the sandbox to swing with friends or roller skate on the parade grounds.

The first day the rains came, Skookie found some chalk and drew a hop scotch on the concrete of the balcony. She, with several of her friends, played there for hours. The second balcony, overhead, protected them from the rain.

About this time, I realized that my little sister would benefit from the same nurturing that made

Alcatraz special to me. All of the adults cared for all of the children. When I wasn't there to watch her, every adult who saw her was looking out for her. If she misbehaved, any adult nearby would correct her. She was being cared for.

We got into a routine which included dinner at the same time every evening and talking around the table. Pop would join us when his schedule fit ours. Now our dinner table included my big brother, Harold, Bobby, Betty, Pop and I. We had long lively conversations. It was great!

We were a family.

SUMMER OF 1953

My friend Nancy and I had met the first time when I was in the fourth grade at Sherman School. At lunch time, we would play tag, or basketball, or hopscotch.

When I transferred to Winfield Scott school, we did not see each other until

we met again at Marina Junior High school. We were in different home rooms, but often played together at lunch time.

As soon as we got to high school, we tried to have PE together and share the same gym locker. She was really good at basketball. She often threw from the foul line and made a basket. Although she was only about five feet tall, she had learned how to jump high enough to reduce the height issue.

Her mom worked as a waitress to support her three children. She and her older sister, Joan, traded Saturdays staying home to care for her little brother, Curtis.

School was out for the summer. Both Nancy and I had to stay busy during the week days. Saturdays were the days we did things together. These Saturdays were busy with brand new things to do.

Nancy had known Marty for many years. When he joined the Navy, he introduced her to one of his Navy buddies, Jack. This young man and his friend, Charley, were stationed on the U.S. Navy ship the "Boxer," at Treasure Island.

It was the first Saturday of summer vacation. Marty's friend, Jack and his buddy, Charley, were both stationed on Treasure Island.

I had ridden the streetcars to Nancy's apartment during the afternoon. We spent the time together cleaning her apartment. Around six o'clock in the evening, we showered and changed into our dressy clothes, nylons and high heels for the evening.

Around seven o'clock, Jack rang the door bell and we went down the stairs to meet on the front porch. On the very first date, Jack and Charles wanted to go to a place down Highway U.S. 1 from Sutros where, they had heard, a country music band played.

My date for the evening was Charley Anson from Toppenish, Washington. He was tall and good looking.

The place was just beyond San Jose. We danced until about eleven o'clock, then went back to the city. By that time, everyone was hungry, so the guys drove to Mel's Drive-In, just east of Market Street.

We had hamburgers and Coke. The car hop fixed the tray to the front driver's seat window. About half an hour later, the car hop came to take away the tray and collect money for the food. Jack and Charlie gave her a good tip.

Jack then drove back to Nancy's place and after getting her phone number, he walked both of us up to her door. We had already explained that neither of us kissed "good night" until after the third date. Nancy used her key to unlock the door. We told them what fun we had had, then walked up the stairs to her kitchen.

We dated Jack and Charley every other weekend while the "Boxer", an aircraft carrier, was in dock.

On our next date, we went to a dance hall up on Market Street, where they had live music. That was another fun night. The band took request. "Harbor Lights" was our favorite. They ordered drinks for us, so Nancy and I were both drinking alcohol. We knew to take it slowly.

Around eleven o'clock in the evening we left the dance hall, and went to Mel's Drive-In again. We probably ordered the same thing. Then Jack drove us to Nancy's place, where we, again, said our good nights.

During the weekdays I did babysitting for some of the parents on Alcatraz. I also had a few housekeeping customers. I could sympathize with working mothers who did not want to clean house on their days off.

I also cleaned Mr. Levenson's apartment every three months. He was a bachelor who lived in "A" building, just outside the fence. The apartment had a very small kitchen, with a table that could be set up after the meal had been cooked. He left dishes to be washed. On the right wall was a couch that pulled out to make a bed. I always changed the sheets on that bed. I could tell the sheets had not been changed since my last visit. The bathroom was also very small. It had a shower with a curtain. The sink had a medicine cabinet just over it, so he could shave and do his grooming.

Mr. Levenson usually left dirty underwear, used towels, uniform shirts, dress shirts and other washables lying around his apartment. I always filled out the laundry list and put the dirty stuff in a laundry bag, to be washed at the prison laundry. He paid very well for my work. He hired me about every three months.

After doing dinner at home with my family, I would go visit the Trudsons, or Jim and Blanche Hudson and their little girl, Sylvia.

On the alternate weekends I still had my friends on Alcatraz.

The weekends were saved to visit the Shumaker's basement at the top of the Island. Mr. Shumaker was the EMT for the prisoners on Alcatraz. He and his family lived at the top of the hill, right next to the Warden's house.

Soon after they arrived on the Island, the teenagers got together on the week-

ends to clean their basement. Along with old discarded furniture, there were old light bulbs that had burned out and were not replaced. In one of the rooms, we found an old table with room for six place settings. The old floors were covered with linoleum.

There was a lot of dirt on the floor. As we attempted to mop the floor, the dirt turned to mud. One of the teenagers brought a mop from home. We found a faucet just outside the back door. We took turns mopping the floors. Gradually the floors got cleaner and cleaner. When the floors were clean enough, we sent the mop home with the kid who brought it.

When all the rooms were clean, we had a meeting to decide the activity for each room. The room with the table would be the card room, where we could play Rummy or Poker or Twenty-One or any other card game.

The big living room became our dance room with radio music to dance to and an old couch to relax on. The stairway to the home upstairs was just off the dance area.

We all agreed not to smoke, because the people upstairs would be bothered by it.

Janet and Gene were about a year apart. Janet was in my grade at Galileo.

Gene was a freshman. They both made friends easily.

We still spent a lot of time out on the bench, talking and smoking. The view of the cities around the bay was beautiful at night. The sounds from the

ALCATRAZ: My Home Town

San Francisco North Beach area came very clear over the water to where we sat.

We could hear the band playing at the dance in the Aquatic Park building. The

cars were very visible going up or down the hills. If one honked, we could tell which car it was. The bells from the Catholic church, in the North Beach area rang clearly and, on some evenings, we could even hear the fish salesmen on Fisherman's Wharf.

Only two weeks of summer vacation left. Mom and Pop Fishers son, Jack, came home on leave from college. We dated often in the month he was home. I began to have very strong feelings for him. On his last night on leave he gave me a little stuffed puppy for a gift and named the pup "Aphrodisa". At the same time, he asked me to write him often and so I did.

I wrote to Jack about once a week for the greater part of the year. He responded regularly. Summer ended way too soon for me.

Diane, 2nd from left. These are some of the children I baby sat when I was a teenager.

ALCATRAZ: My Home Town

Diane Peacock (middle, back) in 2018
with her family.

SENIOR YEAR AT GALILEO HIGH SCHOOL

Soon enough summer vacation ended. Bobby was a grade ahead of me. He now had a girlfriend, who lived in town. He went to work after school to deliver flowers for a florist in the Marina District. He spent most of his earnings keeping his car running.

It became very clear that my mother liked him and did not like me. She would sign his report cards with out any comments. In this Senior year, for him, he received five "Ds" and one "A". The "A" was in ROTC. I signed my own report cards and nobody seemed to notice.

I went to school on the 7:25 boat from Alcatraz. There were several of us who walked up the hill together. The group included Janet and Genie Shumaker, Brian and Tom Severson, Bobby Orr, Don Hurley, Donnie Martin, Agnes Roberts, Bud and Barbara Hart and others whose names I have forgotten.

My friend, Nancy, would meet me in the gym, so we could get credit for taking the class. We played with the basketball, or anything else we could do to get credit for the class. Then we did the other classes required for graduation.

During the second lunch time, she and I left the campus together and took the trolley car down to Market Street. She worked at an insurance company nearby, while I worked at the Bank of America. (It had been the bank of Italy for the first years of business, then WWII came along and the bank changed its name to Bank of America.)

My job was labeled "batch clerk" which required I checked the paper work of the tellers to make sure their paperwork matched the paperwork I had done from the sheet of paper each turned in with their figures on it. That year taught me that I should never work in a bank.

One of the tellers, a guy who had dropped out of the priesthood to go to work at the bank, had a crush on me. He was a really nice guy, but I could not return his feelings. Smoking was not allowed in the bank building, so I had to wait until I got off work to smoke. Banks closed at 3 PM in those days. Those of us who worked there usually were not able to leave until the work sheets balanced. No one was to leave until all the paper work balanced. Most got off around 3:30. I was seldom able to leave until after 4 p.m.

On Christmas eve, that year, the bank closed early so the employees could spend the evening with family. We all went to the bar next door to the bank so we could have a Christmas eve drink with our fellow workers. As we sat in the booth, each of the employees bought me a drink when they ordered their second drink.

Lad Compton (right), one of the "Island" guys I dated. When he got out of the service he lived on the island with his family. For a while he managed the canteen on Alcatraz.

The result of that drinking made me more than a bit drunk. When one of the women tellers husband came to pick her up, she offered to have her husband drive several of us home. I asked him to take me to the place where my friend Nancy lived.

A few years after I left that job, computers would change all of that.

My first cigarette of the afternoon was usually on Pier 4. Most of the time, I took the 5:30 PM boat back to Alcatraz. On that Christmas eve, mother was on the balcony watching for me. When I got close to her, she asked why I had missed the earlier boat. I made some excuse that had nothing to do with alcohol.

I worked at the Bank of America every weekday until New Year's day. After the new year began, I still went to work every week day until the week of graduation, when I turned in my resignation.

She would be on the first balcony watching to see who got off the boat, the "Warden Johnston." Bobby was usually on the seven o'clock same boat. As often as I could, I sat outside on the circular bench at the back of the boat. There were days when the water was too rough to allow women and children to set out back.

I set the table for dinner, then called Pop and Skookie for dinner. She saved a plate full of food for Bobby to eat when he got home. When dinner was over, I went out to visit our friends on the island.

Our high school would be out until the day after New Year's Eve. As was typical of dinner, since She remarried Pop, dinner was three cans of food. She bought canned goods from a wholesale store that sold cans of food with the label missing. It was not unusual to have two of the cans be the same food.

Pop and I would have great conversations when Pop ate with us. When Pop was working or sleeping, She did not talk at the table.

After dark, our group of teenagers did go Christmas caroling inside "B" and "C" building, over at the big duplex on the east side of the island, along the little cottages, and then to the little parade ground.

After the caroling, it was time to go to the Social Hall to do the Christmas play. When the play was over, several of us did special Christmas entertainment.

On my last Christmas presentation, I did my mimic of "I saw Ma-Ma kissing Santa Clause." Don Hurley, Bub Hart, Bobby Joe Orr, and Don Martin sang Christmas carols. They sounded very good together.

When everyone finished being on stage, Santa Claus came into the big room. He did the "Ho-ho-ho" noise that Santa is famous for as the Officer's Club members found him a chair and placed it up on platform made just for him.

The Women's club then organized the children according to age and had the children go get their Christmas candy after each told Santa what he or she wanted for Christmas.

Our graduation ceremony was held at the Opera House on Van Ness Avenue. I did not invite my Her and father because I did not want to hear how much better my brothers' graduation was.

I had made a date with Fred Amendor for after the graduation. About half an hour after the ceremony, a woman approached me and explained that he would not be allowed to date me as he would not marry outside his Portuguese race. I wound up alone, taking a street car to the dock.

ALCATRAZ: My Home Town

It was about this time that my big brother, Harold, asked me to come to his home in San Francisco to help care for his two little children because his wife was pregnant again and about to have their third child. I was excited about getting away from the island.

It was late in August that I had to start the program at Sacramento School of Nursing. She invited my Grandfather, Dr. Ziba Henry, to ride to Sacramento with us. That is when I bid farewell to my old home town.

THE ALCATRAZ
ALUMNI ASSOCIATION

About fifteen years after Alcatraz closed, a group of people who had lived on the Island decided they wanted to get together with old friends and neighbors. They got together and called or wrote to the Alcatraz people to give each a time and date that we would all get together.

At that meeting the Alcatraz Alumni Association was formed. Officers were voted in and the decision to meet every year on the second weekend in August. The officers would have to find a meeting place where members and their families could stay over night as many came a very long way to get there.

Before 1982, the group met on camp grounds in parks. Families would camp out where the kids could play and the adults could visit and catch up.

The state park was near Anchor Bay and the weather was cool. That was the place we met every year until Alcatraz was taken over by the State Park system. Once it became a state park, we could go visit our our old home town.

Sadly, the Native American occupation had destroyed most of our Homes and left trash piles in their place.

The Alumni Association then met in San Francisco and after the meeting, many would visit the Island.

Ranger John welcomed members of the association and had groups listen to the talks and visitors found it exciting. Several of our members would guide visitors to the Social Hall and the lighthouse. Retired officers would lead the visitors through the prison and explain the cells and explain why some prisoners were in tougher cells.

In 2018, Ranger John told us we would no longer get on the Island for free and would no longer be expected to show sight seers around.

I would like very much to thank Chuck Stucker and John Brunner, from the Alumni Association for the pictures which appear in this book. In my heart there will always be an Alumni Association, as the Alcatraz Alumni Association is no longer active.

CONCLUSION

Alcatraz was closed as a federal prison in 1963. Within a year of the closure of the people who had lived there, formed the Alcatraz Alumni Association. We began to get together every year on the second weekend of August.

There were several hundred of us during those first years. We camped for two or three days in Deer Wood Park near Guerneville with a big group of people who had lived on Alcatraz. Some of the non-campers would stay in a motel in the little town nearby. We were still meeting there until 1973, when I lost track of many of my old friends.

In 1969, Native Americans occupied the island. They claimed they had been given the right to occupy Alcatraz in the Treaty of Fort Laramie. During their occupancy, they destroyed most of the living quarters. It was often cold on Alcatraz. They used the hardwood flooring from the apartments and the wood from the cottages to make fires so they could warm themselves. Many left of their own accord.

The remainder were removed on June 11th, 1971 by the Coast Guard.

There is no natural water supply on Alcatraz. When we lived there, the water barge arrived once a week to fill the water tower.

When I visit my old home town, there are still members of Native American group there selling souvenirs or to talking about the occupation. I still feel a bit of anger that they destroyed most of my home town.

In 1972, Alcatraz became a place to tour. It was about that time that the Alcatraz Alumni Association began to meet in San Francisco. I love seeing my old friends, and visiting the island for several hours once a year. As long as I can, I will return to Alcatraz for the homecoming weekend.

In 2017, during our regular visit to Alcatraz, on the Alumni weekend, I got to visit with a woman who was a diaper baby I had cared for when I was in high school. She is now a married and a grandmother.

I'm sure the memories of living on Alcatraz will be with me for a very long time.

Haroldene "Dena" Henry Freeman

www.ingramcontent.com/pod-product-compliance
Lightning Source LLC
Chambersburg PA
CBHW070546010526
44118CB00012B/1237